Storytellers' True Stories About Love

Volume 1

Edited by

Anne E. Beall & Judi Lee Goshen

Chicago Story Press, Inc.

*To Storytellers everywhere who are brave enough
to share their stories*

Table of Contents

Introduction | Lessons about Love by Anne E. Beall

When we decided to edit a book of true love stories, we were unprepared for the response. We received many submissions that described love for romantic partners, children, parents, friends, pets, careers, and passionate interests. We touched a nerve. And it's not surprising. Love can be intoxicating, overwhelming, heartbreaking, and perplexing.

We believe stories are the guideposts we use to navigate our lives. The stories in this volume have much to say about love. They describe why it feels the way it does, how it occurs, and they give insight into how it changes our thoughts and propels us to do things that are irrational and even heroic. The stories we selected touched us deeply. We laughed, cried, and thought about these lovely stories long after we read them.

Many of the stories described the feelings you have when you discover someone who truly understands you and connects with you in a way you have never felt before. These are the experiences where you truly see yourself in another person. These stories described love for friends and romantic partners. The profound impact of that love still reverberates for these authors in the form of gifts they received from that relationship.

Several stories showed us how love can lead to heroic acts. In two stories, parents fought for their child's life and emotional wellbeing in ways that were extraordinary. In another story, an older brother protected his younger sibling from falling into a dangerous crevice and put himself in grave danger—all because of love. That feeling existed for his brother long into their adulthood and middle age. And one author described going to Cuba and entering a building under construction to experience a part of her beloved father's history.

Other stories showed that love often occurs with people one would not expect and in ways that are difficult to describe. In one story, a man described loving a woman who could not reciprocate his love in a traditional heterosexual way, but their love was an important and defining moment of his life. Another story described a deep love and peace an elderly nun gave to a doctor who befriended her. For some authors, love came in the form of a romantic partner who wasn't the person society would choose for them. In one story, a woman fell in love with a much younger man who shared an interest in music with her. She had given up on love when he entered her life and changed it completely. And one man fell in love with a woman his culture absolutely did not understand or approve of, and his journey toward marriage and family acceptance provides many lessons.

For some people, the love of a career or passionate interest propelled them to pursue and experience worlds they would never have known. One woman recounted how she wanted to be a scientist but was discouraged by a college physics professor. Her heart belonged to science and her journey with it was truly one of love. In another story, a passionate artist discovered a taxidermied lowland gorilla in the basement of natural history museum, which led her to do research on him and eventually to celebrate his life with children who visit the museum. For some people, sports teams take a huge part of their heart. One man's story about the 1969 Cubs deftly described those powerful feelings that get revived from time to time. And one author's love of skating forever changed his experience of his family and his community.

Many stories described the heady and overwhelming experience of love—whether it is for a parent, a romantic partner, or a brother one hasn't seen because of the pandemic. They encapsulated the impact of a specific person and what that individual meant to them. One author described what it was like for his father to come home when he was a child, and how much he loved every aspect of his dad—from his whiskers to his shoes. In another story, a boy comforted his mother and tried to show his love for her after his parent's divorce. The depth of these feelings is not surprising; after all, our first loves are our parents.

Other stories painted a vivid picture of first crushes that children have, and the intensity of this sweet and guileless experience of childhood romantic love. In many cases those feelings led to behaviors that were funny, as a couple of authors described, but they may also become a template for love that is consulted in later years. We were struck by how hopeful children are when they love another person, and how childhood romantic love is no less intense than the adult version.

Many of these stories showed how love transforms one's view of oneself. One writer learned that the love for a pet changed the labels she used for herself, and ultimately helped her identify and feel grateful for her life. In another story, love caused an author to become an award-winning salsa dancer. By day she was a psychologist, but at night she was a salsa queen, with two completely different wardrobes.

Several writers also explored the tough experience of losing a beloved. In several stories, the death of a parent, partner, or friend gave authors a greater understanding of the relationship and of the person they loved. And for many, death did not sever the connection; it just changed the nature of it. As a result of these difficult losses, several writers developed a profound, new understanding of love.

We can't talk about this emotion without mentioning one of the most difficult aspects: unrequited love. One author saw the humor when her partner would not commit, whereas another woman eventually saw how the decision to commit to a love relationship created a life she didn't foresee or even want. Another writer vividly painted the complex dance she engaged in with a romantic partner who wasn't available. Her words speak to anyone who has been in love with someone who can't reciprocate, and these stories show us how to navigate some of the more difficult aspects of this emotion. They wisely reveal the people we should run from and those whom we should let into our lives—our hearts often know what is best.

And last, but most important, several stories explored self-love and how essential it is to have a healthy and accepting view of oneself. Without it, we are forever diminished in our ability to love others, and we will be relegated to relationships and situations in which we are not valued.

At the beginning of this introduction, we included a quote by Eckhart Tolle about how loving is seeing yourself in another. When we read these stories, we saw ourselves in all of them. They had important lessons about the nature of love, and they helped us understand our lives more fully. We wish the same for you.

Chapter 1 | Zipless by Arlene Malinowski

This is what we're reading in class: "The zipless was more than sex. It was an ideal. Zipless because when you came together, zippers fell away like rose petals, and underwear blew off in one breath like dandelion fluff."—Erica Jong

Soft-core porn dressed up as Feminist Literary Criticism? Oh my God! I love grad school. It's the 80s. I listen to Blondie, wear parachute pants, and my hair is focused on one simple concept: volume. I am young. I am tan. And I am aware, even as it's happening, that I should be living the perfect summer.

I'm talking about my class with the nice guy whom I work with in the dorms. It's our job to enforce quiet hours and make sure the students don't do anything stupid, like throw a burning couch out of the window of a high-rise. Which they did, twice. It's a lot of paperwork.

"This book says that a 'zipless' is defined as a sexual encounter for its own sake, without emotional involvement."

The nice guy smiles. "Where do you get this stuff?"

"It's Fem Lit by Erica Jong. She's fabulous and very famous."

The nice guy sighs, "I'm in the wrong major."

I continue, "you know what would make this a great summer? *I* could have a zipless. It could be my feminist statement in support of all the women who have suffered under the tyranny of the patriarchal double standard."

He laughs. "Like the brochure says, summer school—where learning meets life."

The truth is, for all my bravado, I am lonely—bone-crushingly lonely. Only a few months before, I had been plopped into the Midwest from Jersey to go to grad school. I know big hair and malls and "going down the shore," not this tiny college town that has a Farm and Fleet store and a flying ear of corn as a mascot. But the university offered me a full ride and a stipend, and the coveted *designated* parking space is like glitter on a stripper. I brag to everyone that it is, "the bookish girl's version of the army."

For my zipless endeavor, I decide to stick to my standard menu of bad boys. The older, sophisticated James Bond type is perfectly dressed in a navy blazer and an Izod with the collar popped. We meet at a Ramada Inn hotel bar in the afternoon for very unfettered behavior. We drink Manhattans, and he caresses my knee, but when I realize he is incapable of forming a sentence without the words, "me," "my," or "I," I pick up my unfettered backpack and go to my Data Analysis and Regression Class, even though attendance isn't mandatory.

As the long days of summer putter along, I hang out with the nice guy a lot. He is smart-smart and makes me laugh. We eat together, go out drinking, and he even cleans my apartment. I feel grateful to have such a good friend. One night, while we are scraping the vomit from the elevator, I tell him, "I've eye-lured three candidates."

"What is the eye-lure?" he asks.

"It's from an article in Cosmo magazine called, *How to Be a Man Magnet.* Step one: Make eye contact and smile. Step two: Turn away. Then three: Look back and hold for a count of one, two, three, four, five. Once, I accidentally did it to a blind guy and his dog on the quad, and if it worked on them, it will work on anybody. Anyway, here's the unfettered update: James Bond was too self-absorbed, so I've moved onto the Brazilian painter."

The nice guy stops. "The one who lives out of his car for artistic integrity? He's gross. You said it yourself."

"I think he's dirty in a sexy kind of way. He wants to sketch me."

"I'll bet."

"What? I'm going to lie on a chaise and say, "Quiero tu carne. Tu carne esta muy caliente. Oh wait, I have to learn Portuguese, right?"

Then the nice guy sighs, "you're too good for them." That's when I see it. He doesn't want to be my friend. He wants to be my boyfriend. I don't want a boyfriend. He isn't my type. He is nice. I don't like them nice. I like them Italian, dangerous and, if possible, from Brooklyn. The nice guy is as dangerous as lint. Besides, he is two and a half inches shorter than me, and I have twenty pounds on him, which means no matter how skinny I am, we will always look like Kermit and Ms. Piggy.

I decide not to spend as much time with the nice guy, but he turns up everywhere—the laundry room, the parking lot, outside the women's bathroom at the Student Center. I do not tell him about the hot bartender who is studying for his GED, but only part time and on the side.

One morning, as we're leaving the dorm because some idiot has pulled the fire alarm at 3:00 am, the nice guy corners me. "Let's go out to dinner." He sounds happy and hopeful. There's nothing worse than a happy, hopeful, nice guy moon-pieing over you. Then the nice guy tries to give me the eye-lure.

I think to myself, *Oh crap*. Now I'm going to have to give him the "I'm really flattered but I don't want to ruin our friendship" talk. Why do nice guys always do that? Why do they ruin everything by being so nice?

For dinner, he chooses a hometown, homespun version of TGIF, complete with the looney outfits, kitschy buttons, and suspenders. This *is* fine dining in the town of the flying ear of corn. He wears brown polyester disco pants and a brown silky shirt. He looks so happy that I don't have the heart to tease him and say he resembles a little turd.

I make sure we go to dinner on a Tuesday night. Not a date night. I order baby-back ribs with extra BBQ sauce. Not date food. I not only eat my plate, but I eat some of his, and I order the double chocolate lava cake and make no pretense of sharing. Definitely not date behavior. We talk and talk and laugh until I am snorting. This isn't time for the "It's me, not you" monologue.

As the nice guy goes to pay the bill, which is my only concession to the date rule, I see my hot bartender tossing bottles in the air and catching them to the delight of his patrons. I think, *with talent like that, who needs a GED?* I strut up to him, a woman burning with defiance, grab his striped suspenders, and purr, "I'll meet you at close." Then I give him the eye-lure and he eye-lures me back. *God, it really does work!*

Later, the nice guy and I sit on the loading dock behind the dorm. The night air is hot and humid, and my skin glows in the shallow yellow streetlight. We are silent, too silent. The "talk" is coming, and we both know it. He sits on the step above me, idly playing with my hair, and shivers pass through my body, igniting a thousand goosebumps. I feel us breathing together. My brain starts buzzing. *No, no, no! He's a nice guy. You don't do nice guys.* But my heart is racing, and that irresistible pull is tugging, tugging, tugging.

As I turn my face towards him, I think, *if I kiss him now, will I ever get him off my back?* He pulls me close, and it is all sweet mouths and hot, salty necks. And just as I am about to say, "Give me a minute to shave my legs," he pulls away, puts his hands into his pockets, skips down the stairs past the dumpsters, and quietly murmurs, "I'm the happiest man in the world," and then he disappears into the darkness.

It was the sexiest night of my life.

I often think about that nice guy and wonder. I wonder what time he'll get home from work and what we're going to eat for supper.

***

Why did I fall in love with the nice guy? I don't know. It might have been his pheromones or something to do with my menstrual cycle, or maybe my higher self was finally speaking to me. Perhaps it wasn't my doing at all. Maybe this turn was a magic spell or a wish that he made once upon a star. What I do know is that things were always easy between us even when they got hard, not unlike the comfort of slipping into a pair of well-worn jeans that fit perfectly.

I loved that he was quietly thoughtful, kind beyond measure, and smart in ways that I could never be. He had a dry sense of humor, listened before he spoke, but most of all, he was one of the last gentle men like my father. I always teased that he was the guy you called in the middle of the night when you ran out of gas... and had a body to hide. But when he held my face and kissed me, all the things I loved about him as a friend suddenly turned romantic. I saw him differently and somehow I knew it was going to be us, together. I was ready to marry him in two weeks.

Ironically, the nice guy has confessed that he kissed me that night because he thought I was a bad girl. He still does.

***

As an actor, playwright, and teaching artist, **Arlene Malinowski** views her solo work as an artistic extension of the social justice work, she has been committed to for the last twenty-five years. She has created shows that she has toured across the U.S. and internationally. Arlene is the recipient of a fellowship from the University of Illinois at Chicago's Department of Disability in the Arts, an LA Theater Ovations Award, and a LA Garland Award. She was a finalist in New Plays from the Heartland and a semifinalist for the O'Neill and Blue Ink Award. Two of her works were commissioned by 16th Street Theater.

She has also worked as an actor in film, television, and theater (Chicago: Goodman, Victory Gardens, 16th Street. LA: HBO Workspace, The Court, Blue Sphere). She's been a visiting artist for the Quad Cities Arts and Artist in Residence at 16th Street Theater. She is a Resident Playwright at Chicago Dramatists, where she developed and teaches the Solo/Story curriculum. As a storyteller, she has performed throughout Chicago. Her work appears in *Paramanu Pentaquark, En Posse Review, Huffington Post, Chicago Storytellers From Stage to Page*, and the *Women of Letters Anthology* by Penguin Press. She is currently touring with her solo play, *Little Bit Not Normal*, which is designed to create dialogue around the subject of mental illness. Her website is: arlenemalinowski.com

Chapter 2 | Bah Dah by Bridget Schank

"Trip trap, trip trap, trip trap, trip trap, went the bridge as the first youngest billy goat crossed. 'Who's that tripping over my bridge?' roared the troll," said my mom with her playful voice that danced around the curtain in Jack's hospital room and greeted me at the doorway. Jack giggled. It was 6:30 am., May 9, 2011. My eighteen-month-old son, Jack, would finally get a new liver today from his father and my husband, Tim. This surgery was a living organ donation that put both my husband and son at risk and wasn't guaranteed to work.

"Now, I'm coming to gobble you up, roared the Troll." I smiled despite my raging fear. My parents had the best voices for this story. I stood in the doorway to Jack's hospital room, not sure if I could enter the room. The cot Tim and I slept on the night before was still unmade. The sun was peeking through the blinds illuminating a giant window painting my brother made. Get-well cards and pictures decorated all the walls. A battery powered candle from the grotto at Notre Dame still burned on the nightstand. My lucky backpack from college rested against the wall and had every supply I would need that day.

I had just returned from driving Tim to Northwestern Memorial Hospital where he would donate a portion of his liver for Jack that would be transported in a cooler by van back to Children's Memorial Hospital. I kissed Tim goodbye and told him I loved him as I watched him disappear into the elevator, not sure if I would ever see him alive again.

Nine months. Nine months we had waited and prepared for that day: "transplant day." Last September, the whites of Jack's eyes turned yellow. We had just celebrated his first birthday with a "Go, Dog. Go!" themed party. Our pediatrician sent us to the ER and then Jack was admitted to the hospital. Four days later, five doctors walked into Jack's room.

"I'm so sorry," said Dr. Bass. With tears in his eyes, he continued, "Jack has end stage liver disease, and he will need a liver transplant to stay alive."

Over and over in complete panic and disbelief, all I could say was "What… the... FUCK… are… you… talking… about?!" I looked down at Jack who was playing with a truck on his hospital bed and saw a look on his face I will never forget, as if he knew. He had known for a long time. When you have a child, you create this picture in your head of their future; his first high school dance, college graduation in cap and gown, walking down the aisle to get married. In a flash, the picture we had in our minds started to fade. We went from living in a world of dreams to existing in a world of pure terror.

Nine months. Exactly the length of a pregnancy. And in fact, we were pregnant with our daughter Gracie for the entire nine months. She was born just five weeks before "transplant day" that May. Nine months where I wondered what did I do wrong? I was his mother. I was supposed to protect him! For nine months, I blamed myself. For nine months, I sobbed alone in our minivan at night. I urgently begged and bargained with my God, any God, to save Jack. My primal and repetitive prayer was one word, *please*.

"'Who's that tripping over my bridge? I will come and gobble you up! Well, come along then!' said the biggest billy goat gruff to the troll. 'I've got two horns and four hard hooves. See what you can do.'" My mom was getting to Jack's favorite part of the book. So I just stayed in the doorway.

Jack loves this book. We had it laminated so we could clean it in the hospital. On the last page of the book, there was a picture of the third billy goat gruff kicking the ugly troll off the bridge and into the raging water. The Troll throws his fist in the air and curses the billy goat. Whenever we read this part, Tim loved to add extra dialogue. We told Jack that the troll was saying, "Damn you Billy Goat! DAMN YOU!" Then one night, when Jack was eight months old, when we got to that part in the book, Jack raised his fist and said, "Bah dah!" Yup, his first sentence wasn't, "I want water," or "I love you." It was "Damn you, Billy Goat!"

Tim and I had so much fun with that.

"Honey, I burned the bacon. Bah dah!" "Ugh… Clogged the toilet again… Bah dah!"

When Jack was diagnosed with liver disease, that "Bah dah" became our battle cry. "Damn you, liver disease! Damn you!!"

Our favorite nurse appeared as I stood there watching my parents and Jack. It was time. I gently touched the door frame to Jack's hospital room, whispered to myself, "Game on." At that moment, I had never been more grateful for my totally insane high-school basketball coach. He always said when we ran out of the locker room and crossed the sideline onto the court, "Nothing else matters than the game. Set all emotions aside and focus on the task at hand." And it worked. We won. A lot. This day was the biggest game of my life. There was no room for anything else. I took a deep breath and walked into the room.

"Trip trap, trip trap… trip trap…" read my mom slowly and in a deep, menacing voice. For all his other surgeries, Jack rode in a hospital bed through empty back hallways reserved for kids going to surgery. This time, they let me carry him. I gently picked up his tiny body with his giant bloated abdomen, its sheer size the result of his dying liver. In one hand, he held his little brown stuffed bunny. I propped him gently on my hip so I could look right into his eyes. One nurse pushed the IV pole along behind us. Jack waved goodbye to all the nurses. As we walked through the hallways, he jabbered about the clouds and rainbows painted on the walls. He imitated the sirens he heard outside, and he patted my face with his chubby little bruised hand.

When we walked into the surgical prep room, the nurse closed a curtain around us so I could say goodbye to him. I tried to hide my tears from him, so I gazed at the medical team's feet circling around the bottom of the curtain as their voices grew more urgent. The curtain opened. At least ten doctors and nurses gathered around us. The main anesthesiologist reached out for Jack. I held my son even tighter.

From behind his surgical mask, the doctor confidently said, "The whole A team is in town for this one. We've got this. They have done this hundreds of times."

But that meant nothing to me. When I handed Jack over, I knew it was out of my control. I looked into the doctor's eyes like I was trying to give him all my mommy powers to help him protect Jack and ordered, "Do not let him die."

Jack waved to me as they walked through the Surgery Department double doors.

Then, for twelve hours, we waited in a small waiting room with very few windows. My mom, dad, sister, brother, and their spouses set up camp in the corner of the waiting room. They were my team that day. Tim's mom, dad, and sister kept watch at Northwestern Memorial Hospital while Tim was in surgery at the same time. My family circled the chairs like covered wagons. They set up a small table in the middle of the room, complete with every magazine, snack, and our Notre Dame grotto candle. It was an altar of distraction. I sent minute-to-minute updates from my computer to all the family and friends who had helped carry us with their love and support for the past nine months. People from all over the world. Even the monks in Tibet added Jack's name to the prayer flags in the Himalayan mountains.

Around lunchtime, the transplant coordinator came into the waiting room and said, "So, the piece of Tim's liver is finally here. Jack's entire liver is out and now we're just waiting to put the piece of Tim's liver in."

We affectionately nicknamed the piece of Tim's liver 'Ted.' I turned to my family and jubilantly said, "Ted is in the house!"

After twelve hours, the transplant was over. Our surgeon, Dr. Superina, sat with me and walked me through all the details. My mom and her best friend, Vicky, along with my dad, sat with me. Dr. Superina had giant brick layer hands and bushy eyebrows. He resembled a Muppet—A giant bad-ass Muppet who had done the first pediatric liver transplant in the early 1980s. Tim and I joked he was even more bad ass than Chuck Norris. And we told many Chuck Norris jokes about him, which made the residents and nurses laugh.

"Dr. Superina isn't afraid of the dark, the dark is afraid of him."

"Chuck Norris wears Dr. Superina underroos."

After we finished talking, it was time to see Jack in the ICU. We went down the hall with dim lights and beeping alarms. It seemed to be straight out of a horror movie. We climbed into isolation gear. I gently touched the frame of the door and walked into the room. It was dark except for the seven IV poles and blinking monitors. The nurses had placed Jack's favorite Notre Dame fleece across his tiny body, and they propped his little brown bunny against his armpit.

All I wanted to do was pick him up and never let him go. But I could not. He was in critical condition, and all I could do was hold his little fingers. His eyes were swollen shut and his stomach was bandaged with forty-seven staples. A breathing tube kept him alive. I placed my hand on his forehead, kissed him, and whispered, "You did it, buddy. I love you so much." I wanted to stay, but I also had to see Tim, so I drove to Northwestern Hospital.

I made the long drive down Lakeshore drive. When I walked into Tim's hospital room, he was sitting in a chair. A tube came out of his nose and drains stuck out of his side as he drooled. He was asleep. I collapsed into the chair next to him and cried. The relief to see him alive was overwhelming and a wild nausea overcame me. I ran out of the room and straight down the quiet dark hallway to the first garbage can I could find and vomited violently. I desperately wanted to expel every image of that day so these memories would not forever be seared into my soul. I hugged the sides of this trash can, gagged, and silently screamed. Seeing Jack and then Tim like that—two of the people I loved most in the world—made me feel I had never been more alone in my life. How was I going to take care of them and our newborn Gracie all by myself? How would I survive this challenge? How would we all survive this situation? I went back to Jack's ICU room and slept on my little cot next to him. In the morning, I opened my eyes and saw Dr. Superina standing next to the ultrasound monitor. The camera wand disappeared in his giant paws as he scanned and scanned until he found what he was looking for. I jumped up, grabbed the screen, and pulled it closer to my face in utter disbelief. "Is that what I think it is?"

Dr. Superina smiled and turned up the volume knob, "Let's listen."

The room filled with a squishing and sucking pulse. Rythmic and steady and strong. There was 'Ted,' the piece of Tim's liver working in Jack. Jack's new liver. Dr. Superina smiled and said, "This is good, and he has a long way to go."

Moments later, Jack moaned in pain. Not from the ultrasound, but from the morphine. Jack was unhappy. The moaning grew louder. I recognized that sound: it was the sound of a body clinging to life. My grandpa made that sound when I was eight years old, and I held his hand as he died. I panicked and screamed for someone to help Jack. Our brilliant young nurse instructed, "Go get some air," and I obeyed.

I stumbled to a bench outside the entrance to the hospital, put my head in my hands and let the tears quietly stain the sidewalk below. I didn't have a Kleenex, so I used my shirt. And that's when I saw it: a hearse pulling up to the front of the hospital.

Someone's child had died that day. And I thought, would Jack be next? It was all too much, and I went numb. Slowly, I walked past the hearse through the revolving door, gently touched the door frame and whispered quietly, "Game on," and walked back down the hallway to be with Jack.

On the seventh night, they moved Jack from Intensive Care to the Liver Floor to continue his recovery. I carefully held him on my lap, and we read the *Billy Goats Gruff,* and I sang to him. Then, I turned on his favorite movie, *Cars*, and made sure he had his bunnies. I was exhausted and crawled onto my cot next to his crib.

I woke up to something hitting my back. I tried not to open my eyes, but something hit my back again. Was I awake or asleep? I rolled over and slowly counted each hole in the ceiling tile above me. I heard nothing because I wore earplugs. Then something hit my back again. I just wanted to sleep. Out of the corner of my eye, I saw the glow from the Cars movie illuminate the room. It cast a giant shadow of my tiny Jack in his tiger gown up onto the wall and onto the ceiling. I took out my earplugs and sat up.

Jack had raised his little bruised hand as he gripped one of his bunnies, scrunched his nose, knit his eyebrows, prepared for war, and screamed as loud as he could, "Baaaaahhhh. Daaaaahhhh!"

He threw another bunny at my head.

"Baaaaahhhhhh. Daaaaahhhhhh!"

I caught my breath. Then he started running around inside his crib. Laughing and bouncing. Shouting triumphantly, "Bah dah... Mommy!!!! Bah dah!!!"

At that moment, the dark menacing shadow above him reluctantly faded into the wall. And there was only light. He reached out with both hands to me, and I scooped him into my arms. Every cell in my body sang. Even in the darkness, I could tell that his eyes were no longer yellow and were now white as snow. And for the first time since Jack was born, I finally knew what my son really smelled like. My heart exploded. My newly postpartum body started to sweat and tremble, and I bled again. The small piece of Tim's liver pulsed under Jack's tiger gown against my chest. Tim, Jack, and I embraced.

Jack was reborn. We were all going to survive.

Bah dah, Jack.

Baaaah daaaah!

***

Rabble-rouser, fundraiser, former community organizer, and nonprofit lobbyist, **Bridget Schank** has been telling stories for social change for the past twenty years. In 2011, she chose to stay home full time when her son, Jack, had a liver transplant.

Bridget's deepest held values are to care for our brothers and sisters every day in every way and to fight social and economic injustices. Bridget is currently the president of the nonprofit, Arlington Cares, which provides funds to help families pay rent, bills, and other expenses in an emergency. She is also actively engaged in supporting several other nonprofits, including Teen Parent Connection and North Star Reach, a camp for children with life-threatening health conditions.

She loves to travel, but hates to pack, has played women's football at Notre Dame, and bakes a mean strawberry rhubarb pie. Her husband, Tim, often warns people about her sixth sense, which often borders on witchcraft. Bridget has performed at storytelling shows including First Person Live, Truth Be Told, The Moth, Soul Stories, Story Sessions, Story Collider, Fillet of Solo, and Universal Sound. Bridget lives in Arlington Heights with her husband, Tim, daughter, Gracie, son, Jack, and her aggressively affectionate golden retriever, Corby.

Chapter 3 | Rich City Skater by Jacoby Cochran

I remember the first time I fell in love, like it was just today. Uh, no, it was not with a person. It was with two bad ass leather boots with marathon plates attached at the bottom and four boneyard wheels on each. It was the grand opening of Rich City Skate, a Black owned skating rink in the South burbs of Chicago. I was standing at the edge of the floor, preparing to get on as the music of James Brown, the godfather of soul, filled the building. You see, I'm a Black kid from the South Side of Chicago. I've been roller skating my entire life. It's in my blood. I grew up skating at all the local skating rinks. I'm talking about the rink on 87th street, Glenwood, Markham, 76th street, Lynwood. And now at Rich City Skate. I'll be honest, I didn't really have a choice when it came to being a skater growing up because my mother is one of the greatest skaters in Chicago history, which means she's one of the greatest roller skaters of all time.

Everybody knows "Sweet Tee" in the skate world. And my siblings and I were lucky enough for her to pass down a few of her talents. As I'm staring out on the floor, my mother whisked by me, the intro to James Brown's *Payback* is her soundtrack. And the minute I heard it, I knew it was my time to jump on the floor, join my mother, and get down. And right as I went to lift my foot and place it on that beautifully stained hardwood floor, my father grabbed me on the shoulder and said, "Hey, somebody just took a shit on the men's bathroom floor, and I'm gonna need you to go clean that up."

You see, a few months earlier, my step-grandparents decided to buy a skating rink. Olympic Skate World became Rich City Skate and immediately my father became the general manager, and my mother became the CFO, aunts and uncles became employees, and my brother, sister and I, well, we were on shit detail.

I'll be honest when they first told us about it, I thought this sounded like a kid's dream, a skating rink to ourselves filled with basketball hoops, ping pong, unlimited pizza, hot dogs, and nachos. Honestly, I thought this is the life, but I quickly realized working with your family is not all it's cracked up to be. It becomes your entire life, especially when you're turning a hobby into your hustle. My siblings and I were forced to learn how to do everything. We had to learn how to clean the skates, sell the skates, fix the skates, and build skates from scratch. We had to learn how to buy the food, cook the food, serve the food, clean the bathrooms, run the gift shop, strip the floor, sand the floor, polyurethane it, dust mop and wet mop it daily. You really can't do those last two out of order.

Within months, we knew how to do every single task necessary to run that skating rink. And we probably spent less than five percent of our time actually skating. And my mom decided I was going to be her little accounting apprentice, which means I couldn't even get the cool job of skate guard, which basically means you get to skate all day while kind of making sure people are safe. No, she moved me into a small office where I had to learn how to use all the accounting software, how to take money, process the receipts, how to store everything in the safe, how to enter everything into the computer. It was at this job that I learned responsibility and discipline, and over the next two and a half years, my family and I spent every waking moment inside of that skating rink. I remember the summer we decided to close it to renovate, to really turn it into our own place.

Those were some of the best years of my life. And ironically, I have the injuries to prove it. I've dislocated the thumb on my right hand multiple times. I've cracked my ankle in three different places and have irreparable damage to my shin. I've torn the meniscus in my left knee, dislocated my shoulder, and ripped my groin on two separate occasions.

Yet, when I think about those years, I rarely think about the injuries. The connection with my family over those first few years was amazing and you could tell that the skate world was energized around another Black owned skating rink in the city. There are not many around the country, despite being a well-known safe haven for Black Americans, starting back around the Great Migration.

Eventually, I had to leave the safety of my family's little establishment. As I grew up, graduated, and went on to college, I stayed very close at first because I couldn't imagine not being able to come back to skate on weekends or holidays. And when I came back during my freshmen and sophomore years of college, it was like nothing had changed. The kids were a little bit older, but the energy remained vibrant. My family was still close, tight knit, and driven. But as I said earlier, running a family business is not without its flaws. I remember starting my junior year of college. As the visits home became less and less frequent, every time I'd come back, things started to feel a little different. That was around the time that my mother decided she didn't want to be involved with the rink anymore. And she left the skating rink for good. After that, the energy just wasn't the same. The initial wave of support and joy slowly started to fade. And the reality of running a small business really set in. I remember coming back my senior year of college and hardly recognizing the place. The smiles that were often sitting on my family's faces had been replaced with frustration and annoyance.

I stopped coming back as often. I moved to New York for a few years and honestly, I didn't even skate for a while. Every time I laced up those bad leather boots, all I thought about was the disillusion of my family. I moved back to Chicago in 2015, a full six years after I left, and the rink was unrecognizable. We couldn't afford to turn all of the lights on and play every single speaker. There was a constant leak from the roof that was starting to damage the floor. Everybody looked tired and drained. I remember thinking before one of our amazing summer national parties,

Maybe there is a chance that if we rally the community, if we remind ourselves how much we enjoyed getting on that floor with one another, that maybe things would be different. But I was probably kidding myself.

The national party at Rich City Skate happened annually, and it was an absolutely gorgeous affair. Skaters from all over the country and world came to show off their skills, and every place had their unique set of moves and style. In Chicago, we skate the JB's. You can catch us low shuffling, big wheel, hitting the curve.

But around the country, you'll find an assemblage of some of the coolest moves you can do on four wheels. I'm talking New Jersey and New York trains, which is a long train of skaters moving together. Kentucky throws, Baltimore snapping, Atlanta jackknife, Texas slow walks, which are just a slow cool step routine across the skate floor. St. Louis ballroom, Detroit open house, where the skaters pick up speed then slide across the floor in the same direction, but their skates are sideways. You've got the Philly fast back, the Ohio stride and gorgeous bounce. Watching people represent their hood made us all feel so tethered to one another.

As we rounded out the roll call, finishing off with the Chicago crew, I watched as my stepfather walked to the middle of the floor and grab a microphone. Honestly, I didn't think anything of it. My dad loved to give speeches. He loved to be at the center of attention, motivate, and inspire. Even make the crowd get a little emotional. When he picked up the microphone, he thanked us all for being there and spoke about what the last ten years as the owner and operator of Rich City meant to him. He then announced to the entire building that it was going to be our last national party. After years of struggling to continue Rich City Skate, he was going to be closing its doors.

I honestly didn't know what to say.

As I looked around, it was clear that nobody else knew what to say. As I looked around the building, all I could see were the images on all the walls of the last ten years of our life, my brothers and sisters dressed as clowns and in SpongeBob costumes, my mom, a ringleader, moving smoothly across the floor. That building represented a place for African Americans. Many of our greatest historical and social figures were hung all around the building; a decade of stories told in Polaroids.

It was like we were all losing a home that we grew up in. It was in that building that I learned what it meant to work hard. It was in that building that I learned who I was. I found my style, my confidence, and my voice inside the walls of Rich City Skate. As individuals started to slowly pack their bags and belongings, they poured out somber hugs and tears. I did something I hadn't done in years. I went to clean the bathrooms. I collected the skates, cleaned them, fixed them, and put them away. I helped to dust mop and wet mop the floor in the correct order. And before everyone exited the building, I asked my dad for a favor. I just wanted one more moment on the floor by myself. So I laced up my beautiful leather boots. And my dad walked into the DJ booth and turned on the godfather of soul. And for one last time in that building, I got down to *The Payback*. I knew even as the doors closed, I would always be a Rich City Skater.

* * *

Jacoby Cochran is a writer, educator, and storyteller from the South Side of Chicago. He is the new host of City Cast Chicago, a daily news podcast about all things Chicago! Jacoby has been featured by The Moth Mainstage, PRX's *Snap Judgment*, and The Museum of Contemporary Art. He is a communications instructor at City Colleges and DePaul University, hosts elaborate cooking events, and coaches public speaking and storytelling workshops across the nation, most recently with Google, Literacy Chicago, and Cook County Jail. Jacoby loves his circle, his city, and his camera.

Chapter 4 | Confessions of a Salsaholic by Maureen Riley

Dirty Dancing changed my life. I knew, watching Patrick Swayze lift Jennifer Grey high into the air, then slide her slowly back down the front of his body until she was kneeling at his feet, that I too needed to be lifted and freed by the God of Dance.

Divorcing my husband and determined not to be depressed, I shell out $150 for red Latin dance shoes and sign up for Beginning Sexy Salsa Class.

Alejandro, our black mustachioed instructor, lays it all down: "I can teach you the steps, but I *can't* teach you how to *dance*. Dance is about passion, erotic sexual passion. You either have it or you don't. You'll have to find that out for yourselves".

I'm looking in a wall-to-wall studio mirror, nine rows deep with Puerto Ricans and Mexicans nearly half my age. Eyeing the curvy Latina next to me, I'm thinking, *she's got it*. And the guy in the skintight jeans in the back row has definitely got it. I'm just not sure *what* I've got anymore.

"Ladies, keep your arms soft as spaghetti so the man can signal his lead through your palm. But remember—until *he* moves *you*—you don't move."

"Yeah—you wait for me," a young blood hoots out. Women hiss, snapping their fingers.

A former feminist radio show host, I plan my exit, because this is macho crap! But oh my God, Alejandro is waving me up front to join him—for a demonstration!

My arms are stiff as dried spaghetti.

"Relax," he says, "just let me have you."

Appalled and not trusting a man to lead me anywhere, I step back. "I can't. I gotta sit down."

He offers his hand again. "How 'bout you just follow the rhythm of the music with me?"

Embarrassed, I step back into the embrace. He smells of Old Spice, like my dad.
Suddenly, we're dancing. And it's amazing.

"Gentlemen, the woman is the picture, and the man is the frame. Your job is to make *her* look good. Now partner up," he says, twirling me back into line where I stand facing my next legal drug: Armando Flores.

As Alejandro calls out the basics—quick, quick, slow, rock step, and close—Armando smiles and slips in two advanced twirls, trying to impress me. And he does. We're discovering the glue that's going to keep us together: we have perfect rhythmic sync.

"You're over dancing the rhythm," Alejandro warns.

Two hours later, we're making out in the front seat of Armando's 1952 Buick LeSabre. I know enough Spanish to understand, "Era bailarin de la calle," means, "I was a street dancer in Mexico." His father took him out of school when he was twelve to build roads and keep him out of the gangs. Basically, Armando was crawling when I was learning how to drive and prepping for a top-ten university. He wears a gold crucifix, is Catholic, and one of seven children—like me. And that's where the similarity ends.

"You work?" he asks.

"I'm a psychotherapist."

"Psychologia? Wow. Tiene un novio?" (Do you have a boyfriend?)

"No. I *had* a husband."

"Ohh." Armando pulls away. "I'm sorry for you."

Several seconds of silence follow.

"So… what are you doing with a little Mexicanito like me?"

It's a good question. It's the right question. I *could* tell him I'm skirting a black hole of depression, dancing for my life, but I don't share my feelings anymore. They're in the deep freeze of my body. Instead, I surprise myself by saying, "I just want to dance, make love, and eat great food. Nothing else. I just want to have fun."

He drives me home in silence.

That night, unbeknownst to me, I make drunken love with a virgin. And in the morning, I have a dance partner! It's hard to get any good at dancing without a steady partner. I figure it's better he doesn't speak much English—that will cut down on any fighting. Dance will be our language.

We meet several nights a week to watch bootleg New York club videos, copy the hottest moves, and commit them to memory by naming them. One day, when Armando blanks on the lead, I suggest, "Do the 'Twist and Fly,' then 'Open and Slide Through the Backdoor.'" Ignoring me, he yanks on my arm aggressively and keeps repeating his same move over and over, boring me to death, until it dawns on me: I'm being punished. I've violated the machismo code—I took the lead! I snatch my arm back.

"Hey! How do you say *asshole* in Spanish?"

A typical partner conflict. Oh my God, did I say *partner*?

I consult a psychic, Selene, who lays out cards and explains, "You had a past life in Peru. His family moved away to find food. You were twelve and never consummated the relationship. Now let him feed you." I am stunned. A week ago, Armando had asked if I had any Peruvian music to make love to—and I did!

As we craft a routine to take to the nightclub floor one day, I teach Armando English, and help him open a bank account to establish credit. He loves to feed me—homemade tortillas, grilled flank steaks, and lots of salsa.

Finally, after six months of classes and living-room practice, waiting for Armando's annoying perfectionism to end, he lifts me up in the air and says, "Put on that little red dress. We're going *out* tonight!" Nightclub virgins, this was our public debut. Club Intas! Around the curves of a long mahogany bar, on black leather barstools, in stilettos and sequins, Latinas hoping to dance sit next to old Cuban gents, slick Puerto Rican street dancers, and new Latin dance school students.

We kick off our street shoes, open our black dance shoe bags, rummaging for the brush. Scraping the stiff wire bristles back and forth to raise the suede nap on the bottoms of his black and white patent leather shoes, and my sequined t-straps, we get ready to turn, quickly and smoothly.

The horns in the ten-piece band blow. Armando stands. His chin and right leg begin to bounce, marking the beats in the music. He points his arm dramatically out to the side, showing off the ten-inch drop of his white, toreador-sleeves. I lift the hem of my ruffled red skirt, and swishing it side to side, shimmy, then crook my finger 'Come Hither'.

Hand over heart, Armando shakes his head and smiles, "Pinchy loquilla, (little crazy girl) you could kill me."

I laugh. We play. I'm happy again. Depression is a frozen stillness, and I am melting. Hot and bare, with a sweet sweat, the cool breath of the horns blow to the congas.

We're out five nights a week now, official 'salsaholics.' My closet vibes seduction. Modest wool skirts and sweaters get shoved further back to make room for jewel-toned cocktail dresses: the flippier, or shorter and tighter, the better. Therapist by day, salsa queen at night; I live a double life.

But maybe there's a bridge. In opening my heart to the music, I've recovered an innocence, freedom, and sensuality life had stolen. To dance *is* to heal. Myself. In learning to partner dance, I've accidentally discovered relationships can be centered in pleasure, not pain.

Although a factory foreman by day, at night Armando is a king of the dance floor. Latina women eye me. I stole one of their men.

"Does that gringa think she can dance?" I hear them say behind my back.

"Ohh Armando, would you teach me that turn?" The women ogle him, seek him as a dance partner because, unlike other men who get wrapped up in their moves or lost in your cleavage, Armando's eyes never leave the woman he is dancing with. His expression ranges from intense to delighted, alive with pleasure in the give and take, in the chemistry of the dance. I am the charmed center of this circle of energy. "La reina de salsa," he calls me. His salsa queen.

I'm wearing a red dress with a twirling carwash hem the night the band plays our favorite song, *Lady in Red*. Armando takes my hand and escorts me confidently, not to the usual dark edge, but to the very center of the dance floor.

As I raise my arm for the embrace, his hand shoots out and grabs my hip instead, leading the turn from there. Delighted, I go spinning across the floor. He travels with me. Circling me like a planet, he calculates exactly where my body will land in space. Deftly catching me around the waist, he pulls me in close, and then, very slowly bends me over backwards, brushing the floor with my hair.

I pray he won't drop me. Choosing to trust, I let him have me.

The crowd explodes, "Juera, juera" (blonde girl, blonde girl). Armando's index finger languidly traces a line down the center of my chest. He circles me in a wide, slow arc, from left to right, and when I lift my leg to lock it around his waist, he raises me back up again.

The crowd thunders applause as Armando whispers in my ear, "Yeah, you've got it."

I am no longer the woman in Sexy Salsa Class who once wondered if I could really dance.

That move wins us $500 and two tickets to Mexico in the 1997 Jose Cuervo Dance Competition. By then, five springs have come and gone. Armando has grown from a boy into a man, and I have found a sensuality, freedom, and embodied joy I have never fully experienced.

I am now ready to trade my salsa crown for the dream I'd left behind.

Lady in Red is playing on the car radio the day I have the courage to say goodbye.

"I'll always love you. You know that right," I say, choking back tears. "But I have to go now. Maybe I'm too old and it won't happen, but I want a baby. This is my last chance to meet someone and try."

He turns off the radio. As we watch the sun slide down the sky to her knees, Armando takes my hand, and in near-perfect English says quietly, "Let me do that with you. We'll move away to a little town where nobody knows us and start over."

My heart crumbles. "No, amor. Remember what I said the day we met?"

Armando lets go of the hand he's held for so many years and puts it over his heart instead. "You are right, Maureen."

I lean over and press my hand over his, trying to keep it from breaking the way mine is.

But I know something Armando does not: it takes more than feelings to make a life work out.

We remained friends. Armando performed and taught salsa lessons. I never had that child, and two car accidents stopped me from dancing. Yet, in going beyond the fear of loss, which is the fear of feeling joy again, my own spirit had risen to meet me. Travelling into its creative, vast, and wild unknown healed me of a deeper divorce—and re-united me with an inner partner. My Soul. With whom I am dancing forever.

***

Cited in *Who's Who of American Creative Women*, **Maureen Riley** is a storyteller, award-winning poet, writer, and filmmaker. Maureen produced, directed, and edited the five-time, national award-winning docudrama, *The Road Home*, broadcast on PBS. Her one-woman show, *Give Me Space in My Time*, produced at Chicago's Chopin Theatre and recent solo show, produced by Second Story, was applauded by WBEZ as "best around town." Her Poetry CD, *Bonfire Heart*, with music by pianist Robert Irving, formerly of the Miles Davis Band, is available at CdBaby.com. A winner of many awards for poetry, she has published in *Columbia Poetry Review, Private Arts Magazine, Nit and Wit Magazine, No Roses Review,* and *Sparrowgrass*. At Northwestern University, she produced and hosted the weekly show, *A Woman's Place* for WNUR-FM radio. She has studied with renowned healers and shamen and is a transformational life coach and medically certified Master Energy Healer (www.purelyvital.com). Her clients have included Celine Dion and her dance company. She is currently writing a book about her near-death journey into multidimensional reality where, beyond the reach of medicine, a brain tumor was miraculously healed.

Chapter 5 | The Oneness of Time and Space by John Hahm

My sister is calling me at three in the morning. Our brother Wendell has had a heart attack. He's resting now, after they put three stents in his arteries. We almost lost him. The conversation ends.

"Damn it, Wendell," I scold him in absentia. "Can't you ever get it right? I'm your older brother! I always go before you! You're not supposed to go before me!"

I fall into a vertigo, with nothing to grab onto. The years and miles no longer separate Wendell and me.

My kid brother Wendell and I are back on that forested hill behind our house in Hawaii. I'm ten, and Wendell is seven. I'm telling the little guy a scary story my teacher told us, about a friend of his who went for a hike right here in these hills in the Nuuanu valley. He fell through a chasm hundreds of feet deep. He didn't see the hole because it was covered in vines, dead leaves, and loose earth.

"These hills have been hollowed out by erosion in a lot of places," I tell him. It's a school lesson every Hawaiian kid has heard, and every Hawaiian teacher has taught for over a century.

"Ah shaddup! You and your scary stories! You talk like a goddamn book!" he says.

I can tell he's still angry at me for calling him stupid and teasing him for being a slow reader.

"I want to go home!" he yells. "I'm gonna tell Mom and Dad you forced me up here, and they're gonna beat your—"

We freeze in our tracks, spooked by a weird sight just ahead of us; the top of a tree sits there, like the broad-brimmed hat and head of a great gnome, with no torso or legs under it. Edging closer, we see that the ancient tree has fallen through a hole, and only the very top of it is visible from a distance. The gash in the loose earth, the hard black basalt rock cliff underneath is disguised by a lattice work of decayed vegetation, exposed roots, and rotting fruit. And then we feel the ground fall away under our feet, and instantly we're struggling, wriggling, grabbing at tall grass, vines, and tree roots. Wendell is sliding down a muddy gash in the path, and I grab his arm and pull him onto firmer ground. We scramble onto the low-hanging branch of a tree and sit there panting, staring at the gaping hole in the earth, just a few yards in front of us.

I nearly lost my kid brother. We sit there, our heads filled with wordless questions. Wendell looks at me, as if to say, *What do we do now?* I don't know what to tell him. I put my arm around him and rock him back and forth as I wrack my brains, trying to figure out what to do. But I can't come up with anything.

We hear the droning of a power-mower in somebody's yard, hundreds of feet below. Familiar sounds, cold, clammy mist, and flowery, fruity smells waft their way up the hill to us, tantalizing us with the dangerous illusion of normalcy.

"I'm sorry, Wendell," I tell him. "You were right all along."

That's not what Wendell wants to hear. "You dirty crookah!" he yells at me. "Why'd you get me up here then?"

"We'll be okay, I know how to get us home," I lie. "But we can't stay here. It'll be dark, and it might rain. Come on, let's go."

Wendell stares at me mistrustfully, eyes brimming with tears and lower lip quivering. "I'm staying here!" he whimpers.

I grip his shoulders and say as calmly as I can, "Come on, Wendell. We have to walk out of here. It's going to get dark, and it might rain. It's easy," I tell him. "I'll walk in front of you. I'll hold on to some vines, and I'll go from one tree to another. You follow me. We'll stop every so often—"

"We don't know where the holes are! You might die!" Wendell argues.

It's hard to argue with that kind of logic. I jump down and break off a skinny tree branch for a walking stick and start walking. I poke the stick into the earth with my right hand and grab at the rope-like vines and branches with my left. Like I'm sweeping for mines. After a few steps I stop and signal to my brother to follow me. Very reluctantly, Wendell hops off the low branch and follows me. The shadows deepen around us, hiding tough vines and roots that could trip us, hiding the treacherous deep holes in the forest floor.

"One day we'll look back on this and laugh!" I call back over my shoulder.

Wendell says nothing. I think he sees through the bravado. I hear him grabbing at hanging vines, stepping carefully into the shallow depressions in the forest floor, and I feel his fear at every step.

He calls out, "Wait! What do I do if you fall through a hole?"

I shush him screaming, "*You hear that*? That power mower we heard earlier. It's getting louder. We're getting close! Just think of how you're going to be twenty years from now. Think about when you're a rich old man with four kids and a big house in California! The stories you'll tell! You'll tell them about this!"

"Ah shaddup!" Wendell yells at me.

He is his cocky old self again. I can tell he is embarrassed about crying back there. He sounds more confident now.

"You talk like a goddamn book all the time, you know that? Ahhh! You're so slow!" And he tries to push past me on that uncertain ground.

I grab him by the scruff of his yellow Snoopy tee-shirt, and I roar at him. "Hey! I'm your older brother! You got that? I go first! You don't go before me! Now get back there! Or I'll beat you up right now and leave you here!"

He looks up at me, his wide eyes brimming with tears again, and right away I feel guilty again. It isn't his fault we're in this jam.

"Ah, Wendell, I'm not going to do that. Let's rest a while. You hungry?" I reach into my backpack and find only my sketch pad notebook. Wendell reaches into his and hands me a tin of Vienna sausages.

"You stole dad's Vienna sausages!"

We laugh, and we eat. We talk about where we'll be in 2000, in 2017…

"I'll be richer than you," Wendell teases. "I'm the smart one. I brought food up here. You brought your stupid notebook."

We laugh again. We are brothers again. We get up and walk back down the hill, Wendell trailing me close on my heels.

"Look, what's the difference between swimming in five feet of water and swimming in a hundred? None. You just swim, that's all!" I say, proud of my little aphorism.

"You were dumb to get us up there," Wendell reminds me. "You should have known better. My friends say you sound like a book."

"Like I care what your little kid friends think," I tell him.

He throws a rotten guava at me, and its mushy wetness catches me right in the back. I throw one back at him, and the air is alive with rotten guavas. And we're laughing so hard!

Ah, yeah… But…

Wendell has had a heart attack. He's resting after they put three stents in his arteries. I'm rubbing the tears out of my eyes. And I look up and I see my kid brother Wendell sidling past me on the treacherous mountain path. His baby-faced frown is comically at odds with his yellow tee shirt, with Snoopy doing his happy dance.

"Hey, little guy," I tell him, "You don't go before me. I'm your older brother. I go before you. And… what do you mean, I talk like a book?"

***

John Hahm grew up in Honolulu, Hawaii, and got his MA in English at Northwestern University after a stint in the US Navy. He recently retired from teaching at Northside College Prep High School, where he coached the Academic Decathlon Team and took student groups to Europe on spring breaks. These days, he's taking tango lessons and would love to re-visit Buenos Aires. But his love of storytelling is his prime passion. He's been learning from some of the best writers and tellers in Chicago.

Chapter 6 | Daddy's Home by Lou Greenwald

Just hearing my dad's car in the driveway made my entire body jump, my mind electrify, my heart pound, and my eyes pop open wide. This was my extraordinary, exciting, ecstatic, happy life, and this was love. I never used the word love when I was a kid. I just felt it every single time I saw my father when he was walking toward our house, sitting in the kitchen, playing the violin, or sitting on his brown chair listening to Beethoven or Bach. There was always an anticipation of touching him, grabbing him, and him holding me. His clothes were a special fabric I could hold on to and smell. And he always allowed me to feel the warmth of his legs, arms, and face. Always.

I did not see anyone else. I don't remember my mother as much as a child, but I can remember the smell of my dad's cigarettes and his unique smell. I recall the whiskers on his face that I would rub with my cheek, his "sandpaper," and his slippers waiting by the door, which were shiny, brown, and huge. When he walked in the door, I would grab him with all the power of a seven-year-old. Physically, it was a wrestling match between us. I would not let go as he hobbled around the house with me hanging on, feeling his muscles straining to get away. But no, I would not let go. I needed to be physically knotted with him.

When he took off his shoes, I would slip my feet into those boats; there was so much room. These leather replacements of him felt so good on my small feet. My dad would howl with laughter when he saw me walking around in them. I could make him laugh as hard as he laughed when he saw the comedian Sid Caesar on television. I felt proud of my ability to affect him. I loved this power.

Just looking at his face made me happy. His smile of yellow teeth due to all the years of smoking those damn, fucking cigarettes offered encouragement for me, and also seemed to communicate, *Keep going, I'm happy, keep pestering me, keep looking at me, there's more excitement coming, so find out what it is.*

The memories of his possessions, like his fishing rods, his colorful ties, his shoes, and the towels he took from hotels like the New Yorker, are souvenirs in my mind of a once joyous, exciting childhood. His pockets were like caves full of coins, keys, and papers. My hands would dive into his pockets, looking for quarters. Quarters in those days, which was the early 1950s, were real money. A quarter could buy you a hamburger or a milkshake at a drugstore. Two quarters were a fortune.

When my dad was not home, I would go into his bureau drawers, which were like museums to me. I never touched his gun in the top drawer because it was off limits. But I loved holding his socks. And on top of the drawer was his gold watch that had a calendar and stopwatch on the face. It was a Movado watch.

And then there was his violin. Shiny honey-colored wood accompanied by a long bow. It was like a religious symbol to me. He played those strings and beautiful music came out. My mom would play the piano at the same time, and this picture of the two of them together in my house is etched in my mind, as memorable as the *Mona Lisa* at the Louvre in Paris.

Looking back, I realize I was obsessed with my dad. Being with him in his car was better than any amusement park. He would let me sit on his lap and steer his big black Lincoln. His laugh was not far away. This exhilarating experience combined touch, power, smell, motion, and sound. Because of these early rides, I became an expert in naming cars, and I could name a car at night from just its taillights. I felt truly alive for those seven years and ten months of my life.

"Love" for me is the most powerful *word*. So powerful that I misinterpreted what I was feeling was universal for all. I thought this was how the world worked and how people interacted. Love for me was knowing I was accepted, I was allowed to talk, to touch, to wrestle, to sit on a lap, to rub my face and feel whiskers… at any time. No one knew how powerful this feeling was for me. My young brain could not separate my life from love. I truly felt coalesced with my dad, even though the word love was never mentioned. It was simply my way of *daily* life. Love was a thought process, and the electricity produced from touching someone, inhaling their smell, and seeing their approving smile, hearing their accepting voice, and feeling the things they touched, created this intense feeling only I knew. "I love" for me meant "I live."

I also experienced the great loss of love; my father died when I was seven. It took me years to say the words, "He died."

I became paralyzed, looking straight ahead, not laughing anymore, not jumping up and down for anything, not touching anyone. I was like the shell-shocked soldiers who returned from war, just shapes of their former selves. Today, it's called PTSD. All I had left of my dad were his classical records; Beethoven's Fifth Symphony and Bach's Air on the G String. I would listen to that music every day after school because I knew he had listened to the same records. And no one at home or at school ever talked to me about his death. No one asked me how I felt. It was as if a surgeon sliced away emotional parts of me and left me with tears ready to flow.

Paralysis and emptiness are what happens when love is lost. And this pain cannot be easily shaken. I would sit on a bench staring at the clouds blow by while the other kids laughed and played. I would sit in a classroom looking at the teacher moving her mouth up and down, but I didn't hear anything.

I understood loss so well that when I became a therapist, I had no trouble feeling my clients' pain. The pain surrounds a heavy mind and one's body feels disconnected. When I tell someone that I understand how they feel when they lose a lover, it is the truth. Decades later, when my own therapist asked me to say the words, "He died," I broke down.

No wonder I dabbled in crime when I was thirteen years old. Cars were a major link I had with my dad. At night, I would "borrow" our neighbors' cars for a few hours without their permission. I knew how to start cars without keys. I would always return the cars, so I truly never stole them. I just needed to feel that car under me, to drive it, to feel powerful again. I was caught one night by the cops and that was the last time I "borrowed" a car.

Lost love became an empty vacuous drawer in my mind. Imagine nothing. Imagine emptiness. It's almost impossible to think of nothing. That drawer used to be filled with everything great. Now, it only contained air. To fill up that drawer would require an avalanche of everything good: sight, smell, touch, thought, electricity rampaging around my mind and body, every great human fantasy.

I learned much too early that nothing lasts. The template of love was in my mind. It had been filled for a short, glorious time. I now know it was an invention of a seven-year-old.

The sight of my dad was like seeing a God; it filled me with glorious joy. Even as a child in Miami, I would not have noticed a hurricane, complete with a torrential wind and leaning trees, if my dad was coming toward the house.

But since his final day on Dec 25, 1951, nothing has matched these experiences.

Daddy's home, his car is in the driveway.

***

Louis Greenwald was a podiatrist for twenty-five years in addition to being a degreed licensed psychology counselor. He spent many years volunteering for the Alliance Against Intoxicated Motorists, Illinois's premier anti-drunk driving advocacy, and was its president for two years. Louis has received many awards and mentions in news articles, including the Chicago Tribune's Eric Zorn Column, People Magazine, WGN TV and radio, and also ABC Television 2020 Television News Show, for his volunteer work assisting victims of drunk driving.

Louis was an original board member of the North Shore District 112 Education Foundation, and he created a successful vehicle sticker program that funded the foundation for years. He is married and has two wonderful children and four cherished grandchildren.

Louis, in the last quarter of his life, has found storytelling as the most expressive of all art forms and tells stories as often as he can.

Chapter 7 | Gratitude by Francesca Sobrer

"Marry me."

This was on our third date. Oh, I know he didn't really mean it, he was just caught up in that moment. That moment of joy, of *let this be more*, "Marry me," he said.

Pep was supposed to be the guy I dated so I could figure out how to date. I was just going to be another woman walking through his busy bedroom.

I first saw Pep during coffee hour at the Unitarian Universalist Church in Bloomington, Indiana. I started going to the church about a year before to meet new people. I had moved to the Midwest from Massachusetts with my two young children and husband, who had gotten a job in nearby Columbus. A lonely agnostic can find refuge in a Unitarian church. I met and made friends with Mary Beth, a vibrant woman my age, who would become one of my closest friends. Through our friendship, I found the courage to leave my unhappy marriage of ten years. I found the strength to take care of my two small children as a single mother. Under the shelter of this liberal, social gathering place known as the UU Church, I was able to come back to myself, to recognize my own voice, the one that speaks from my heart rather than the steady drumming of fear often disguised as practicality in my brain.

It was the voice of my heart that said: *Quick! Turn around, there he is!*

I turned and there he was, looking every bit the well-dressed professor, his dark hair curling just a bit around his neck, a kind face, a sparkle in his eye, a kinetic energy that conveyed movement and stillness. Our eyes met for a brief moment. Pep nodded his head toward me with a slightly differential bow; a very proper but inviting hello. I nodded back.

Over the next week I called Mary Beth, "Tell me about this guy, Pep."

"Oh," she said with an excited wistful sigh, "He is from Barcelona. He teaches Spanish and Catalan literature at Indiana University. He is a real gad about—a ladies' man. I think he might have a girlfriend or two, nothing serious."

He was *very* charming. Given that I was only interested in testing the waters, Pep might be just the guy.

After weeks of mutual furtive glances and sly smiles at the coffee hour in the church's meeting room, Pep asked if I would like to join him to see the movie, *A Scent of a Woman*. I immediately called Mary Beth and told her Pep asked me out. "Oh, I'll take the kids!" she volunteered.

In an effort to declare my independence, I insisted we meet at the theatre. As I was rounding the corner to meet Pep, I sent up a prayer: *Please let me be me and let that be enough.*

He was waiting for me outside the theatre. Our eyes locked, and he bowed his head in the way of an old-school gentleman. His careful manners made me smile. It seemed like all the people in Bloomington I knew were also there at the movies that night. There was a hum, as if everyone in the audience was settling in and saying, "Finally! They are on a date!" More than once, Pep made sidelong glances at me.

After the movie, we went out for a glass of wine, which ended up being a champagne special that came with two free flutes as part of some promotion. "Well," Pep said, "a souvenir of our first evening together."

I smiled at his optimism.

"In my country," Pep said, "we drink Cava, the Catalan word for champagne whenever we celebrate. To our first date," he toasted. Then we started talking, each sentence easily rolling over the other. I told Pep about my limited dating experience. I had married young and was determined not to drag my six-year-old daughter Greer and three-year-old son Ryland through my dating life. No boyfriend of the month club for me. I was a working graduate student in Theatre Education and could not afford a babysitter, and I wouldn't give up time with my children for a date. I could only go out when my kids were with their father.

"Still interested?" I joked.

The next afternoon, Pep called and said he enjoyed our time together and understood my time constraints.

"So I am inviting you to please call me when you are available." His voice was earnest and kind. His offer to ignore the dating protocol of the man calling the woman was the most charming invitation I have ever received.

After years of listening to all the wrong voices, I moved forward with caution. I could not afford to make a capricious mistake. It wasn't just my heart that worried me; it was the hearts of my children. I had already upended their lives in a determination to have joy in my life. I needed to listen to myself carefully.

Pep had the charm and manners of Marcello Mastroianni, but the mischievousness of Harpo Marx. He spoke with a subtle Catalan accent that made his English sound precise, which suited his poetic professorial demeanor. But there was a playful twinkle in his eye. He would look at me with an eager grin, tell me I was sexy, and then lunge at me like Harpo. But he kissed me like Marcello.

We had little in common. Pep was thirteen years older than me, almost a generation. He was raised in Spain, under Franco's rule, whereas I was raised on the east coast in the unruly 1960s. Born to a small, humble, working-class family, Pep's father was a baker who owned a small bakery in a working-class neighborhood in Barcelona. My family was large, loud, and from certain privilege. Pep was a tenured Professor, now chair of the Spanish department at Indiana University. I was a graduate student trying to reinvent myself, a creative. Pep had been married twice before and was a confirmed bachelor, with so many girlfriends vying for his attention. He wooed me with long phone calls made after my children went to bed and over dinner when my kids were with their father. It wasn't long before we discovered our common denominator; both Pep and I believed that life should be about joy.

We talked, we kissed, and sneaked in lovemaking between classes while my children were at school. We kept talking, our conversations growing ever more serious. Every now and then in a burst of enthusiasm, Pep would declare, "Marry me!"

"Be careful," I said, "one of these days I'm going to answer that question and you may not like my answer."

"You're right," he said, "I should not be so glib about something so sacred."

I moved forward with my efforts to divorce my husband. Pep untangled himself from his girlfriends. All the while, the voice in my heart was humming. After five months of dating, I took an enormous leap and officially introduced Pep to Greer and Ryland. Although Greer was skeptical at first, Ryland was wildly enthusiastic. It wasn't long before our dates went from cozy dinners of two to family picnics of four.

Then one night, Pep proposed. No grandstanding, no declarations, no diamond ring hidden in a napkin, just a straightforward query, the sparkle in his eye now serious. "I want to take care of this. I want to help you take care of your children. Marry me?"

After three weeks of careful deliberation, of long conversations with my heart, I told my brain to take a back seat, and when I was sure, I was sure, I said yes.

On the morning of our wedding day, I woke up, not so sure. I stood in the kitchen of our house, looking out the window and thought, *If I have learned anything at all in this life, it is that I can say no. It doesn't matter if the wedding is paid for, or that the family has come in from out of town, or that there is a beautiful wedding dress hanging in the closet. None of that matters; I can still say no. Because how do I know? How do I know if my yes is the yes*? It was an effort to listen to the hum of my heart over the rattle of my brain. *How do I know if Pep is the one?*

Just at that moment Pep came into the kitchen completely naked. He looked at me with that mischievous gleam in his eye and said, "Today is my wedding day, I must do a dance." He went out into our open backyard and did this ridiculous dance—hopping up and down, arms flailing, looking more like Pan than Harpo, yelling "Whoo-oo! Whoo-oo!"

"Thank you," I said, that is exactly who I want to spend the rest of my life with.

As it turns out, it was the rest of his.

We had a son together. We shared twenty-two of the most joyful years of my life. Pep died of colon cancer seven years ago. A few days before he left this planet, he whispered to me, "Thank you for giving me a family."

"Thank you for wanting one," I whispered back.

***

Francesca Sobrer comes to Chicago via Bloomington, Indiana where she was the director and teacher of North Theatre for over twenty years. An east coaster, she grew up on Nantucket Island, studied acting in New York City, and has a degree in Theatre from Smith College.

Francesca has been fortunate to work in theatre, whether as a teacher, an actor, writer, producer, or director all her adult life. Once she landed in Chicago, she found a place for all her creative outlets in storytelling. Francesca is a Moth StorySLAM winner and tells stories all over the city of Chicago. She has also told stories in Vermont and Massachusetts.

When not crafting the next story, Francesca coaches young actors and storytellers. She still acts when time permits and is a lover of the ocean and travel. Her favorite city is Barcelona, her favorite beach is on Nantucket, and her favorite times are with her three grown children, always.

Chapter 8 | Science: A Love Story by Christa Avampato

Everyone during my rural and very poor small-town upbringing cheers me on through my straight-A school years. I go to state-science competitions and win prestigious academic awards doing what I love—math and science.

I spend most of my childhood outside playing in the mud and climbing trees, unless I'm reading about dinosaurs, my very favorite subject. I'm the only person in my high school to go to an Ivy League university when I enroll in the University of Pennsylvania's engineering school. This is a huge deal for everyone in my town.

"Penn's going to open the entire world for you," people say.

I start with sophomore-level physics. I work hard that first semester and although I enjoy the class and learn so much, I get a C minus. It hurts. Devastated but determined, I go to my professor's office to find out how I can improve, and what concepts I haven't quite grasped yet. He's sitting at his very large and imposing wooden desk in front of chalkboards full of complex equations when I arrive.

"Let me see your exam," he says.

My heart is racing. He's a world-renowned researcher on quarks. He reviews my exam and hands it back to me with a disinterested look.

"So what can—"

He cuts me off, "I can't help you."

"What?"

"You have no mind for physics," he declares.

"But if I could—"

He interrupts me again. "There's nothing I can do for you," he says slowly and with annunciation.

He goes back to his reading as if I'm not even there anymore. I don't say a word. I just gather up my backpack and scramble out of the office. I cry all the way back to my dorm. Science is all I ever wanted to do, and now my mind isn't capable of it. This professor knows much better than I do what I'm capable of, he's an expert.

That semester, I also take required classes in history and economics. I sail through those with A's. I think it's a sign. Science and I just aren't a match anymore. We've grown apart, and it's moved on without me. My mind is made for liberal arts now. It's the path of least resistance. So I take it. I change my major with my academic advisor the next day. I graduate with honors, and a broken heart that never quite heals and never really forgets about science. It is, after all, my first love.

Another love of mine in college is theater. I'm heavily involved in producing and set designing throughout my years at Penn, with a little acting thrown in for fun. That leads me to a career managing Broadway shows and national theater tours. I manage every business aspect of a show: travel, logistics, union contracts, finance, and human resources; it is the greatest business training I could have.

After seven years of eighty-hour work weeks and no break, I'm on Broadway's Beauty and the Beast. One night the showstopper number, Be Our Guest, is in full swing. I'm in the back of the house. The Napkin Girls are twirling around Lumiere, the candlestick, while he sings.

"Be our guest, be our guest, be our..."

WHACK!

One of the Napkin Girls, who's having an affair with the very married Candlestick, punches him on stage in front of the entire audience and he just stops—cold. He's in complete shock. The conductor of the orchestra tries to keep it going, but it's useless. The finale of the first act is completely off the rails. I spend the rest of the evening, long into the wee hours of the morning, in my office as a mediator for flatware.

Back in my hotel room, all I can think is, "What am I doing with my life?"

The next day, I quit. No plan. No job. I go to Florida to spend some time with my sister, and science as a career creeps back into my mind again. My mind that's not made for physics. My mind that always sees science as the one that got away.

In my late 20s, I'm considerably tougher and more stubborn than I was when I was eighteen. I decide now is the time to prove how wrong my college professor was about me. I enroll in an upper-level college physics class, study my ass off, and ace it. A perfect score on my final exam. I do have a mind for physics. I'm overjoyed, jumping up and down with my exam in-hand in the college parking lot, and then absolute dread washes over me. I start crying. What might have been if I hadn't let that college professor take science from me? Now I'm in my late twenties.

"It's too late to start over," I tell myself.

I get a job offer as a fundraiser. The business world is the one I know. The path of least resistance again. I leave science again, right there in that college parking lot. Science and I are a couple of teenagers who have grown up and moved on but have never forgotten each other. Time just passed us by.

My career has a lot of twists and turns but has always revolved around business. Now I'm a Director of Product Development for a tech company. Still, I've never been able to shake science, my first love. I still think about it all the time. Lamenting. Science, I can't quit you.

About a year ago, one of my science heroes, Ken Lacovara, visits New York City. Ken discovered the largest dinosaur ever found, named Dreadnoughtus. We're only Twitter friends at this point, and he asks me if I want to meet him at the historic Explorers Club on the Upper East Side of Manhattan. I jump at the chance. The next day I sit with him in the beautiful Members Lounge, surrounded by artifacts from all over the globe discovered by famous explorers like Sir Edmund Hillary and Robert Peary. We talk for three hours about dinosaurs, science, exploration, and education.

Finally, he says to me, "You're so passionate about science. Why didn't you become a scientist?"

I tell him my humiliating story about the college physics professor. Ken is the only person I've ever told this story because he's the only one who ever asked.

He looks at me and says, "I'm so sorry that happened to you. No one has the right to be a gatekeeper to your dreams. I think you could still have a second act in science if you want it."

A few months later, I'm walking to work listening to the Ologies podcast. The host Alie Ward is interviewing Chris Lowe, a marine biologist who specializes in sharks. He explains that sharks have this mucus that encourages rapid healing after they mate. It is necessary because females sustain serious wounds from the males during mating. The patriarchy is alive and well in shark land, and they blame natural selection.

Now, as a professional product developer focused on innovation, I become very interested in this mucus that causes rapid healing. It could apply to medical innovations. Imagine Band-Aids that promote rapid healing with a gel in them similar to this shark mucus. A few years ago, my boss opened my eyes to biomimicry, a field started by scientist Janine Benyus. Biomimicry is the study of biology and the application of its genius to our human-built environment and products. That shark mucus reminds me of biomimicry. Could I create a product that works that same magic for us that the mucus does for sharks?

I spend the next two hours at my job googling places in New York City where I can take a biomimicry class to learn more about the field. What I find is a new graduate program in biomimicry at Arizona State

University. It's an online, cross-disciplinary program built for working professionals in product development just like me, and ironically Janine Benyus started it.

Science, in true West Side Story fashion, is this finally the time and place for us? Is this our second act that Ken said is out there waiting for us? Somewhere?

That week, I joyfully submit my application. Three months go by with no news. I call the admissions office right before Thanksgiving.

A nice man named Walter says, "Christa, I'm so sorry."

I start to cry a little bit.

"The department's overrun with applications. I'm sure you'll hear something soon. Just keep checking the status of your application online. Okay?"

"Okay," I manage to croak out.

I think he knows they have rejected me, and he just doesn't want to tell me.

Science, I thought we had finally found our way back to each other like two long-lost lovers. We can't get our timing right, can we? You are a Montague and I am a Capulet.

A week later, there's still no news on my application. It's like the guy you're dating who ghosts you with no explanation. He's just gone. I sink into my couch and close my tear-filled eyes.

The only thought that goes through my mind is, please send some magic.

I sit with that thought for a long time. I finally open my eyes and go into the kitchen to get some ice cream. That's what I do when I feel terrible. I meditate, and then I eat ice cream. A lot of it.

I come back to the couch, and the light on my phone is blinking. I have a message from Arizona State University.

It says, "Congratulations on your admission to the Biomimicry Graduate Program. We're delighted that your passion led you to us."

I'm proud to say that I do have a mind and a heart for science. After graduating from the program with a near-perfect GPA, I'm a science expert at the Biomimicry Institute. I've published pieces about biomimicry in well-known science magazines and given many talks about my specialty to enthusiastic audiences of all ages. When I combine my passions for biomimicry, business, and storytelling, and apply it to climate change—the important social issue to me—I know that my friend, Ken, is right; I'm the gatekeeper to my dreams now.

***

Christa Avampato is a writer, product developer, and biomimicry scientist whose career has stretched across Capitol Hill, Broadway theatre, education, nonprofit fundraising, and health and wellness. She has worked for companies ranging from startups to Fortune 500 companies in retail, media, entertainment, technology, and finance. She combines storytelling, business, and science to build a better world for all beings through her company, Double or Nothing Media. Her clients include Carnegie Hall and the Biomimicry Institute.

Her young adult novel, *Emerson Page and Where the Light Enters*, received the Nautilus Book Award, Wind Dancer Films Award, Readers' Favorite Gold Medal, TopShelf Magazine Award, and a finalist placement in ScreenCraft's Cinematic Book Competition, and was featured by Kirkus Magazine. She's written for *The Washington Post*, *Natural History*, *The Henry Ford*, *Ask Nature*, *Pipeline Artists*, and *Inside History*. She's been a speaker at SXSW, Wildlife Conservation Society, Virginia Festival of the Book, Teach for America, Games for Change, NYU, CUNY, Columbia University, Alzheimer's Foundation of America, and Brooklyn Brainery. She was an associate producer for the PBS documentary series *Live at 9:30.*

Christa lives in New York with her rescue dog, Phineas. Crushing cancer during the height of the Covid pandemic gave her endless gratitude, and a renewed sense of joy in the beauty of life.

In late 2021, Christa was accepted into two graduate programs in sustainability at Oxford and Cambridge.

Learn more and follow her adventures at:

https://twitter.com/christanyc
https://instagram.com/christarosenyc
https://christaavampato.com
https://doubleornothingmedia.com
https://emersonpagebook.wordpress.com/

Chapter 9 | Love Never Dies by Judi Lee Goshen

I've heard it said that you're lucky if you have one best friend in your life. But I've had several. There was Reggie. We met when we were twelve. Jacquie, I met the year after, and of course, my high school bestie, Roxy. But having a best friend would take on new meaning in my early thirties when I met Victoria, Vicki.

Victoria was exactly like me. We thought alike, had the same beliefs, the same sense of humor, were both actors, and we were both non-drinking vegetarians. There was no jealousy, an emotion that plagued my previous friendships. Never a misunderstanding or sideways look. I could talk to her about anything without judgment. Victoria was my soulmate. Shortly after we met, I had a reading with a medium who told me that Vicki and I had spent many lifetimes together, helping each other transition to the other side during the death process. I never gave it much thought. All I knew then was how much fun we had, how much laughter we shared. She understood me in a way no one ever had, and I saw a light in her other people could not see. Two sides of the same coin. We were even the same sun sign down to the group level.

When we talked on the phone, I could feel my spirit elevate. She exuded pure joy, and it was infectious. As a child, her mother dubbed her *joy to be around*. I once had an audition for the part of a lesbian and worried about being believable. She responded, "I think touch is touch," and with that, she lightly stroked my arm. It sent electricity through my body, and I smiled.

"I stand corrected," I replied as we laughed. "If I were gay, I would SO steal you away from your husband."

In the movie, *As Good as it Gets*, there's a scene where Jack Nicholson says the most beautiful thing to Helen Hunt about how she is such a great person and how lucky he is to see that. I quoted that in a card to her because we used to exchange cards all the time that expressed our gratitude for one another.

Because we looked alike, we usually had back-to-back audition times. One time we had an audition for a variety show. She slept over in the guest room and we worked on our parts all night.

"She's your competition," my husband scolded. I just laughed.

"Do Piggy for them," I coaxed her. Piggy was a character she made up about a young woman with no teeth who could not speak well because of a tractor accident, so when she said her name was Peggy, people heard Piggy. Vicki didn't need any coaxing. She put her fork down and went into character, her face contorted, and you'd swear she had no teeth. The family roared with laughter. Then Victoria turned to my son and said, "I hear *you* do impressions." My son did one, and we all laughed again. Everyone loved Victoria!

"You are so funny," she would often tell me.

"Me? No. You are," I would always protest.

Years later, I would find that comedic voice and write and perform my own material that would lead to my book, *Fornicationally Challenged*. She saw in me what I could not.

Five years into our friendship, she moved to New York to further her acting career. As much as I encouraged her to follow her dream, I didn't know how I was going to manage life without her in Chicago. I saw her five times a week, and we talked five times a day. However, even when she left, we remained strongly connected. We talked often, and she came back to see her family, audition, and hang with me.

One day, while Victoria was on a set somewhere in California, I got some awful news and couldn't reach her. So I yelled out to the universe, "Vicki, call me now!"

A few minutes later, my phone rang. "What's wrong?" she asked frantically.

That often happened with her. She always sensed when I was in trouble.

Ten years later, Victoria and her husband, Michael, adopted baby Rose. Shortly after that, they diagnosed Victoria with cancer. Stage Four. She called me at work and told me the news. I got through the rest of the workday, but when I stepped into my apartment that night, I collapsed on the floor in violent sobs. Living in separate states was one thing, living in this world without her was unfathomable.

During the next year, I flew back and forth to New York for every surgery, staying with her overnight in her hospital rooms.

One day Victoria said to me, "You know, if I pass, we will still be able to communicate."

"I know," I said, "But it will be really hard on my part. I'll have to meditate, raise my vibrational level. Oy, that's a lot of work." We both laughed.

When the end of her life was near, I quit my job, rented out my apartment, and went to live with her and Michael in New York.

My family was shocked. "You quit your job?!"

"It's Victoria." My only explanation, but they didn't understand.

I took care of Vicki for two months, bathing her, dressing her, and trying to get her to eat—something—anything. I kept my emotions in check. Between her needs, the needs of a four-year-old, and all the household chores, thankfully there were always tasks to keep me occupied. Sleep came easily from pure exhaustion. But I knew I was where I needed to be. It just felt right to be there.

One night Michael, Vicki, and I were watching TV as she channel surfed. She needed a distraction from the pain. She stopped on *As Good as it Gets*. We were right at the part where Nicholson says to Hunt, "I might be the only person on the face of this earth that knows you're the greatest woman on earth… the only one who appreciates how amazing you are… and I watch [people] and never get [they can't see that they] just met the greatest woman alive…"

Victoria cried, and I cried. I went to her, and we hugged and cried as Michael wondered what was happening.

She died on a Sunday surrounded by her husband, me, and a few close friends. I brushed her hair and filled in her eyebrows before they took her body out of the house. That night, Rose slept at a friend's house, and we all got drunk.

Before the memorial, I went back to Chicago to see family. I needed to be in a place where I could mourn. In her house, it didn't feel like I could openly mourn my loss because it was nothing compared to a child losing her mother and a man losing his beloved.

When I arrived at my daughter's home, I realized I left my computer in the airport bathroom. Frantic, I called the airport, put in a claim online with United, and as I was running around, Victoria's picture popped up on my phone. Was that a sign that everything would be alright? I didn't know. All I knew was that everything I had ever written in the last ten years was on that computer. No back up. Several days later, Michael and Rose came to Chicago to see their family, and we planned to all drive back to New York for the memorial. The night before we left, I got a call from United. They found my computer! We picked it up the next morning on our way to New York and I held it on my lap for hours. Thank you, Vicki.

On another occasion, Michael sent me to buy a booster car seat for Rose. When I got to the store, the shelves were bare. They lived miles away from major stores and I didn't know where else to go. Strolling the neighboring aisles, I hoped to find something, but they had sold all the booster seats. I sent up a wish, *Come-on, I need a car seat for your daughter.* I went back to the aisle that had been empty and found one lone booster seat, complete with the cup holder that Rose wanted. "Thanks, Vicki."

When I returned to Chicago, I slept with the blinds open because there was a twinkling star so close. I stared at it and said, "Hi Vicki." The following month, the star was farther out in the sky. "Wow, you're moving up." The last time, when I turned out the light, there was an intense brightness in the room. I opened the blinds to see the moon, low and brilliant. "Well, now you're just showing off," I said with a laugh.

Four months after Victoria passed, my daughter was pregnant, and I was anxious. She recently had a miscarriage, and I feared if it happened again, she would have an emotional breakdown. I was at work one afternoon thinking about it and left my desk to take a walk. When I came back, a picture of Victoria was on my phone; it was her message to ease my worried heart. Her picture seemed to say, "I got this, Judes." Her smiling, smirky face told me everything was going to be all right. I believed her, and my daughter delivered a healthy girl.

Six years later, I still feel Vicki with me. I hear her advice in my head, and I keep her ashes on a shelf in my home office next to a picture of us taken at the Grand Canyon.

"When are you going to let her go?" someone recently asked. I thought, why would I want to do that? We are all made of energy, and if energy cannot be destroyed, that means Victoria is still with me in a new form. It's like when water evaporates; we can't see it, but science says it's still there. So, no, I will never let Vicki go. Death does not end a relationship; it just takes on a new form.

***

Judi Lee Goshen has a degree in fiction writing from Columbia College. She has written the book, *Fornicationally Challenged: My Reluctant Return to Dating*, (which received a Readers' Favorite Award as well as one of the Top 100 Notable Books by Shelf Unbound). She also co-edited *Chicago Storytellers From Stage to Page*. She has been published in The South Loop Review and Story Salon. Several of her screenplays and teleplays have garnered recognition from Writer's Digest and The Slamdance Competitions.

As a Moth winning storyteller, Judi has written and told hundreds of stories including her comedic one-woman show: *Fornicationally Challenged*, directed by the renowned, Mark Travis. The show had successful runs in Los Angeles and New York.

Judi has been a stage actor since the age of seventeen. In her twenties, she was in an improv group with Steve Carell, and her thirties were spent doing dozens of national TV commercials. Most recently, she portrayed a doctor in Dick Wolf's *Chicago Med*.

In her day job, she works for the University of Chicago Crime Lab and Education Lab, an organization that provides data analysis to law enforcement, city officials, and the public-school system, making Chicago safer and more equitable.

Chapter 10 | Love in Translation by Jitesh Jaggi

I could see Whitney from across the bar, several cocktail-laden tables in between us. She was crying, looking at me with eyes that said, "How could you?"

I smiled back and told our story to a room full of strangers for whom I was Contestant Number Ten, a wildcard entry at a storytelling competition in Chicago. What followed was a few cynical glances, smiles, amused laughter, a collective gloom, some uncoordinated claps, and a winning trophy—in that order. Whitney, my wife, who didn't know I had signed up as a participant, cried throughout the six minutes it took me to reveal our relationship to the world. It was the first time in the two years since we started dating that I revealed our love story to anyone. And it was to an audience of complete strangers.

Secrecy is expected when you grow up in a conservative household. I was born and grew up in India, where children do not share their dating lives with their parents the way Americans do. And I don't mean the intimate details of the relationship, I mean the relationship itself. Parents prefer its existence to be kept private–a sort of "don't ask, don't tell" rule that guards against awkward conversations about an active sex life. Indian parents would prefer their offspring to learn about sex on the wedding day and figure it out along the way as generations prior to them have. It is not something you engage in before signing on the dotted line of a marriage certificate. And if you do, at least pretend you don't. In their eyes, I was a virgin until 2018, at the age of twenty-nine, when we got married.

The only taboo that beats having sex is engaging in it with a foreigner. So, it's no wonder that when Whitney, an American, and I connected on Facebook, and saw our friendship blossom into a deep love, I did not tell my parents. They were unaware of all her late-night *Good Morning* texts that I responded at night to, all the *Love Yous* and the emojis, all the sexting along with steamy pictures that kept our long-distance relationship going, and all the promises of turning this situation into a long-lasting, fruitful marriage.

What my parents saw was that I often had to work late into the night and attend the numerous overseas client calls. I'm sure they thought of me as the greatest customer-care executive who never lost a smile and blushed even when interacting with customers.

I had to maintain pretenses. Not just for my parents' sake, but also for Whitney's sake. She had to battle the perception of millions of Indians whose only contact with white women was through Hollywood films or porn. There are unverified statistics circulating on WhatsApp that claim American divorce rates are much higher than those of Indian arranged marriages. Combine that with incessant movie teasers of the liberated Hollywood heroine, (often in the company of men and martinis), and you have the stereotypical image of American women being *easy*. They appeared as sex-hungry, ultra-modern, feminist witches whose morals are lower than the hem of their micro-miniskirts. Combine this with the Indian obsession for fair skin, and white women are revered as goddesses who also happen to be sluts.

I had seen weddings called off because the parents discovered their offspring's partner belonged to a different caste, even sub-caste, despite a common language, religion, and social class. Although things are slowly changing, marrying an American is still rare. Bollywood movies have plots where the hero rescues and eventually romances an alien. But the idea of a brown man marrying a white woman is too bizarre to consider. An affair? Sure! But only to make the Desi heroine jealous that her man could have a fairer girl, so she better come back to him and apologize. But a lasting, deep connection? You must be at least an eccentric millionaire to get away with that. Even for Indians living in America, it is something that is best avoided. So, for the simple folks back home, an American woman would be most likely seen as an 'extra,' dancing raunchily in the background of a music video, or in a selfie.

Maintaining our secret love soon turned into an adventure. I wasn't allowed to visit Whitney because my tourist visa was rejected *twice*, so we decided to meet in India. The day I brought Whitney home to meet my parents, I introduced her as my client. That role was more believable to my parents in a country whose service industry thrives on outsourced customer-care and back-office operations from rich, developed countries like America.

But Whitney wanted to be a partner, and a daughter-in-law. And she was right. She deserved the acceptance of my family.

When I finally told my mother the truth, she simply said, "I knew it. You think I don't notice the cropped hand on your shoulder in your pictures? And who comes back from a business trip abroad with an extensive knowledge of the country's beaches?"

She was relieved I finally confirmed her suspicions. Apparently, my mother had joined Facebook simply to stalk me. I had been behaving suspiciously lately. She recognized the "fair business lady" leaving a fair number of likes and comments on my posts. But mostly, it was the quiet reverence Whitney held in her eyes when she met my mom, the way no business contractor would look, that gave us away. And it also didn't help that I kept accidentally touching her hands when translating my mother's small talk from Hindi to English so they could communicate.

"She asked, 'how long are you staying in Mumbai for?'" I said to Whitney on my mother's behalf, smiling profusely.

"She asked 'if you found the food okay. And if the air-conditioning is cool enough for you,'" I blushed like an infant hiding a coin in his fist.

My mom and I agreed we were going to keep this between the two of us. Which automatically meant that my dad, my sister, and my mom's sister were also going to know about it. Fine! Between the five of us, then.

Amidst this environment of secrecy, Whitney and I moved in together in Chicago. The visa authorities at the Mumbai embassy knew more details about our relationship than anyone else. In the visa application, they asked us to submit printouts of our call logs and text messages. This practice was done to rule out any suspicions that our relationship was a scam to get me a Green Card. They knew exactly when and how many times we met, the cafés we found cool enough to take pictures at, the sweet names we called each other in our texts—all in the name of evidence.

After two years of long-distance dating, moving in together was now a life where physical proximity was a given, where having your partner close enough to hear them breathing in the middle of the night could be taken for granted. It felt like waking up from a happy dream only to discover that you're now living it.

And out of contractual obligation, because I was in America on a fiancé visa, we got married. This enlarged our circle of confidants to ten people; the judge and our two witnesses, who were Whitney's colleagues, joined by her parents from California on Skype. Now we had everything.

But it still felt like we were hiding. If two people get married in the middle of a drab courthouse, with no extended family and friends, are they really married? We couldn't even post pictures of our engagement rings on Facebook where we first connected. Nor could we share vignettes of ordinary things that couples get excited about; the buying of seasonal plants, the birthday surprises, the quirky ways that one partner has of doing dishes. The secrecy weighed more heavily on her than on me. I didn't expect her to totally understand the nuances of a culture where live-in relationships were frowned upon and seen as too forward.

Because I was waiting on my work permit, I had no money to take her out on dates the way I had during her Mumbai visits. One day, cruising through the internet, I came across a raffle for two free tickets to a storytelling show, one that I had heard Whitney talk excitedly about. So, I entered the raffle and won two free tickets. She looked so happy. And I was so proud.

During the show, the host announced that there were slots available for those in the audience to tell a story. Knowing that I had a performance-poetry background, Whitney nudged me to sign up. I refused because I'd never considered myself a storyteller, even though I'd always told lots of stories. But as I watched each performer on stage, my heart sank. I brought Whitney for a date but couldn't even afford to buy her a drink. I felt like I'd let her down.

So I threw my name in the hat. And in four long bathroom breaks, I texted myself a synopsis of our love story. Whitney didn't doubt my excuse of having an upset stomach because I had eaten Crab Rangoon for the first time the night before. When they called my name to come up on stage, I looked through the corner of my eyes to see Whitney cheer for another participant. The host pronounced my name to rhyme with 'digest.' I got up and walked toward the microphone. It still didn't hit her I was actually going to perform.

I spilled my guts. I mentioned her by name, I jogged through the highlights of our relationship and said it as plainly as I could, which came out all jumbled. I didn't allow myself to look at her for more than a few seconds because I knew I'd choke. I kept focusing on the four or five things I wanted to convey, as planned in those awkward bathroom writing sessions, and filled the rest with whatever came to mind in the moment. Somehow, it sounded cohesive enough for the audience to follow the narrative, and good enough for me to be declared the winner of the competition. At the end of the night, random strangers walked up to her and congratulated us on our wedding, an experience as close to acceptance and validation as I could give to her.

She couldn't stop talking on our drive back home. It was pure exhilaration in that tiny car. I promised her I would consider telling more stories in the future. A promise that I've fulfilled on stages across Chicago in the last three years.

Our relationship is no longer a secret. A month after that performance, I posted a picture of us on Facebook and never looked back. We flew to India the next year and got married in a traditional Hindu ceremony. The best part was seeing her face glow as a long line of extended family members congratulated her. They didn't know our story as well as that small room of strangers who saw me perform, but they could see how comfortable we were around each other. And that was enough. We now celebrate two anniversaries: one on the day we *had* to get married in the Chicago courthouse, and the other when we *chose* to get married in that star-lit venue in Mumbai.

***

Jitesh Jaggi is a recent immigrant from India, currently living in Chicago. He ended his career in finance one day when he lost all the data he forgot to save on an Excel sheet and realized he just didn't care. That tipping point led him to become a writer, and he is currently working on a book of essays. A two-time Moth StorySlam winner and a producer for the Story Collider, he also coaches individual and corporate clients in telling their stories. He loves writing his own bios because he can refer to himself in the third person. Jitesh can be easily bribed with books and chocolates.

Chapter 11 | Beautiful by Nestor Gomez

Every day before I leave my house, I stand in front of the mirror contemplating my reflection and I say, "You are beautiful. You are beautiful. Damn, you are beautiful!"

The first time someone called me beautiful was when I was around eight years old. I was playing dress up with my sister and she wrapped a towel around me to create a dress. She stepped back to look at me and said, "You are beautiful."

At that instant, our father walked into the room and angrily grabbed a corner of the towel that wrapped my body and yanked it away.

"Men are not supposed to be beautiful, men are supposed to be manly. I don't ever want to see you playing this kind of game again," he barked at me.

The reason I was playing dress up with my sister was because I asked her to play soccer with me, but the only way she would play soccer was if I agreed to first play dress up with her. I agreed, and a few minutes later, she wrapped a blanket around me to create a dress.

But my father didn't give me time to explain the situation to him, and he said nothing else. Silence, not talking about things, was the way my father and my family dealt with issues.

A couple of years later, I became very close to my uncle, who was a few years older than me. Because my father never wanted to teach me anything, and never had time for me, my uncle taught me how to make origami figures and how to play with marbles. He was the older brother I never had. I was happy. It was wonderful to have someone who paid attention to me and taught me things. Back then, my family raised bunnies on the patio of our house in Guatemala. My mother often sent my uncle and me to the nearby farms to cut grass we used to feed our bunnies.

One day while we were out cutting grass, my uncle asked me to do a favor for him. I was very shy and naïve, he was the person I was closest to, the one person I could trust and count on. He asked me to take off my pants, lay down, and let him climb on top of me. I let him because I didn't want to ruin the relationship I had with my uncle.

A couple of days later, my mother sent my uncle and me to cut grass for the bunnies, but we were taking too long, so my mother sent my sister to look for us.

"What are you guys doing?" my sister said, when she saw my uncle on top of me without pants. She ran back home and told my mother what she saw.

After that day, I was not allowed to go anywhere with my uncle alone. But my mother never talked to me about what happened. Silence, not talking about things, was the way my mother and my family dealt with issues.

Silence was also the way I dealt with things.

I developed a speech impediment. I stuttered whenever I had to talk to people, especially at school, whenever the teacher called on me to answer a question. I really stuttered when I had to talk in front of the class.

"Your son needs some kind of therapy," one of my teachers who was fond of me, said to my parents at a teacher-parent conference.

"Therapy is only for rich or for crazy people," my father responded. He felt insulted and angrily walked out of the room.

The next day, the teacher called me to her office after class and said a friend of hers was a speech therapist. She talked to her friend about my stuttering, and he said I should practice talking in front of a mirror so I could get rid of the stutter. I nodded. Once I got home, I practiced talking in front of the mirror, but I only did that for a couple of days because I hated to see myself making faces as I tried to talk, but stuttered in front of the mirror.

I hated myself.

It took many years for me to get over stuttering, and from time to time, I still do, but I never went to therapy. I only went to therapy as an adult when I was going through my second divorce after my fifth attempt to kill myself. That is when I finally went to therapy

"So how are you feeling?" the therapist asked me during our first session.

The truth is that when I'm feeling down and someone asks me how I feel, it usually makes me feel worse. I felt like picking up the chair and throwing it across the room.

"This is a waste of time. Therapy is only for rich or for crazy people," I said, getting up to leave.

"Before you go," she said, "can you look across the room and tell me what you see?"

I looked across the room and froze. I hated what I saw. There was a mirror on the other side of the room, and I hated what I saw. I hated myself.

It took many sessions of therapy to finally understand that the sexual abuse I experienced as a child was not my fault; I had just been looking for love and I had been taken advantage of. It took me even longer to understand that love doesn't come from how others see you, or how they treat you, but from how you see and treat yourself. And there's nothing more beautiful than loving yourself. It took a lot of time, but one day I was finally able to stand in front of the mirror and not hate myself.

Now, before I leave the house, I look at myself in the mirror every day and repeat those words that have become my mantra.

"You are beautiful. You are beautiful. Damn, you are beautiful!

***

Nestor "the Boss" Gomez was born in Guatemala and came to Chicago Undocumented in the mid-1980s. He told his first story at a Moth story slam to get over the stuttering that plagued his childhood. Since then, he has won more than sixty Moth Slams and several Moth Grand slams. Nestor has also created, hosted, and produced his own storytelling show, *80 Minutes Around the World,* a show that features the stories of immigrants and refugees from different parts of the world along with their descendants and allies. The show is designed to help us understand the realities, struggles, and dreams related to the immigrant experience and can be heard on a podcast. Nestor has also published a collection of stories detailing his experiences driving for ride-sharing companies, which is titled, *Your Driver Has Arrived.* You can listen to the podcast, buy his book, or learn more about Nestor by visiting his website, Nestorgomezstoryteller.com

Chapter 12 | The Summer of '69 by Steven Hoffman

Love comes in many forms during a lifetime. And the objects of our love vary widely. But is there a greater love, one truer and purer, than the love and adoration we bestow on our sports heroes?

Well, not so much for me. I never felt the tug of professional sports on my childhood heartstrings.

I remember White Sox games were often on the lone TV in our home, and once when the White Sox played the Cubs, I heard the announcement that Adolpho Phillips came up to bat. Except I thought the announcer said, "Here comes a Doubtful Phillips," and I wondered why he was always doubtful. He was an excellent player. I just wasn't interested in a game with players who had such low self-esteem.

Then 1969 came along, which suffered from an excess of positive self-esteem, which the entire city of Chicago caught. Me too. Suddenly, it was easy to fall in love.

I was in middle school and couldn't get enough of the 1969 Cubs. I knew everything you could know about the team. Today, fifty years later, I know nothing about the neighbors on my block, but I can recite without pause, the entire roster of that team by batting order, position, and number. I loved them passionately.

Several times in the spring and fall of 1969, I cut school with my buddy Larry and took the L to see a game. Thirty-five cents for train fare, a buck to get in the left field bleachers—front row, left field bleachers! Maybe another buck for a hot dog, Coke, and popcorn. It was a week's allowance, but worth every cent. It was certainly the best $2.35 I've ever spent to be with the ones I loved.

The memory of that time—the spring days in particular—has never left me. The stunning collapse of the team in the fall hasn't faded from memory either. From a lofty perch at the top of the National League East in mid-September, the giddy fans watched in growing dread as everything collapsed, day after dreadful day. The Cubs lost seventeen of twenty-five games, while the start-up New York Mets won twenty-three games out of thirty. They won the World Series. Nearly half a century would pass before the Cubs would become world champions. As many have said, the story of the 1969 Cubs informs the worldview of many Chicagoans now in their sixties. These beliefs echo in us: never fall too deep. Brace for the fall. There is no God. The world sucks. But even if the world sucks, it's not the fault of Ernie Banks or Ron Santo.

I moved on. Pro baseball, and the team I loved so passionately, were no longer a part of my life. A summer romance at best.

But it turns out that the magic we waited 108 years for was very alluring. And so it was that in late summer of 2016, the Chicago Cubs hypnotically drew me back to the thundering bandwagon. For the first time in decades, I followed the team. Meticulously. Obsessively. And to nearly recapture the soaring feeling of the summer of 1969, I texted back and forth throughout the World Series with my daughter, who was living far away and with whom I had never shared a love of sports. We could share this love because she had jumped on the same bandwagon. And I could join in the sports conversations at work, without my usual cynical contribution: "Seriously? Sports, again? Don't fall in love with things that don't love you back," a melancholy echo of my first disappointment with the Cubs so many years before.

Of course, 2016 ended better than 1969, with a World Series Championship. And it was thrilling. But baseball was no longer the same game. The world was not the same. And those of us who first fell in love in the summer of 1969 could only look wistfully into the past amid the unbounded affection that broke out in Chicago that year.

About four months later, in the depths of yet another dark, dank Chicago winter, I was browsing at a local bookstore. My other daughter, a bright and curious ten-year-old, roamed the store. I stood at a display of coffee-table books about the Cubs and opened one that told the history of Wrigley Field. My daughter walked up at just that moment and asked what I was looking at.

So I told her about this long-ago infatuation. I told her about 1969 and the magic the park has held for generations. I told her how I used to skip school to see them play, and that I would sit with my friend Larry in the front row of the left-field bleachers.

And then I flipped the pages backward, while I said, "You know, I'll bet that if you look at the chapter on 1969, if there is a picture of the left-field bleachers, I'll be in it."

I didn't really believe there would be a picture of the bleachers, but I still flipped to that year in the book. We came to a picture of the left-field bleachers, and I said: "So, I used to sit in the front row. Let's see…"

I scanned my finger across the page to the very edge of the picture. And there I was, standing next to my buddy, arms outstretched, leaning over the wall, trying to snag a deep-fly ball from the glove of the Mets left fielder. I had an intensity of purpose and desire I don't think I've had since.

I was stunned and shouted, "That's me! That's me!"

My daughter thought I was making it up because I made up a lot of stuff. I had previously told her I played for the Cubs, so at best, she was just confused.

We left the store with two copies of the book, one for me and one for Larry, who is in the picture with me.

A print of that picture now hangs prominently in my home, next to classic photos of Ernie Banks and Billy Williams. That photo is a reminder that those days of pure magic, joy, and love were real.

I keep that photo in plain view every day, because it reminds me that hope springs eternal. As does love.

Go, Cubs, Go.

***

Steve Hoffman lives in the suburbs of Chicago and is a novice at storytelling. His most recent attempt at creative writing was in a high school English class in 1972, an in-depth analysis of Great Expectations, a novel for which he read only the Cliffs Notes. After seeing the red lines and corrections on his first draft of this story, he wondered if his middle school years might have been better spent, after all.

Chapter 13 | Surrendering into Love by Patti Shaffner

"Surrender to the unknown and trust that the universe will lead you home."

~Karen A Baquiran

It was August 1989. The man I had been seeing for over three years decided that we should see other people. I was lying in bed at his house staring up at the wooden ceiling. Normally, I would have wanted to know what was wrong with me, but I didn't protest. I lay there finding patterns in the wood while I thought calmly, *Okay. Well, that is that. You know what? I have my children, my family, and my friends. What do I need with a man, anyway? Highly over-rated.*

Every relationship in the fourteen years since my divorce seemed like a battle to remain true to myself with men who said I should do things differently. Everything from how I folded laundry, to how I raised my children, to how I spent my free time. Fine! So be it. I surrender.

That night I visited The Court, a restaurant and bar that featured a jail cell in a dark dining room and a separate bar room with a raised stage. It was a good place to get a burger and a decent drink, and it was the only venue with live music six nights out of seven. Talented, semi-famous musicians on tour often performed there, many from the Chicago folk scene. And then there were musicians like me, homegrown talents, who filled in when no well-known musician was playing. I had been hosting the regular open mics for about six years. The Court was my home away from home. It was where my friends were.

A few weeks later, I came in to do a gig. I hugged my friends, set up, and rolled through my three hours on that Thursday night. At the end of the evening, I walked up to the bar so Vickie, the bartender/booker, could give me my check. My friend John was there with a tall, attractive man.

"Hey Patti! This is my friend Dave. You oughta let him play bass for you sometime."

I handed him one of my business cards. "Sure. Call me sometime."

I thought nothing more about it. The following week, when I was trying to separate my teenaged sons from fighting, my phone rang. It was that bass player John introduced me to, asking when I would come to the Court again. I told him maybe the next night. I went with curiosity.

He was there. Was he waiting for me? Many men were interested in me because I was a performer. I was skeptical of his attentions and intentions. I sat down and got right to the point.

"Why are you interested in me?"

"I don't know. That's what I'm trying to find out."

Well, that s a new one, I thought.

He had only been divorced for a year and was going to nursing school. He was working on eventually living closer to his kids. He also revealed he was eight years younger than me.

"I'm thirty-eight!" I blurted out.

"My last girlfriend was forty!" he replied, trying to sound reassuring.

"I don't want to know about your mother fixations," I quipped, and excused myself to go to the restroom.

Vickie stopped me on my way back. "Hey, this guy is really into you—and he's not gay. I checked."

I agreed to a dinner date with David.

I arrived at the restaurant and met him in front. At our table there was a perfect red rose across one plate and a poem that he had written. It spoke of meeting a person and feeling a sense of recognition.

Ooo, a romantic, said the voice in my head.

We talked about his divorce, his kids, his poetry, my kids, my music, his music, good food, and wine. After dinner, we walked around town and talked. I told him what I wanted in a relationship. I saw myself with a partner playing music, someone who would be honest, intimate, and creative with me. I wanted laughter, joy, surprises, and tears. I thought, *this sounds like a frickin' Hallmark moment.* I said everything I had been envisioning for a long time. I told him that if two people who love each other are going to fight, it should be about something damned important! All that little shit just didn't matter to me anymore. I didn't want to waste time with someone who didn't want the same things that I did.

After walking for hours, we ended up in front of The Court, staring at each other. The local cop circled the block again and again. Each time we were still there, still talking, staring, sizing each other up. Until, at last, I pulled myself away and drove home, buzzing slightly with the hope of possibility but cautious about another relationship. And this one came with kids.

We started hanging out, walking the dunes, and meeting at The Court to listen to music. We grew closer. One night, when my kids were visiting my mother for the weekend, he stayed over. He was talking to me as I was drifting off to sleep in his arms and I heard him say, "I love you. I love you because my heart is not stupid. It recognized you the very first moment I saw you. It said, 'Wow Dave! That one! That one is strong enough and wise, and whole enough to help you heal and remake yourself into the man you want to be.' My heart knew you right away, at first sight. It just knew. It knew that passing such a love would be a tragic mistake. My heart knew what it wanted before I even knew your name."

I snuggled closer into him, taking in his scent as he continued to talk. I heard the rhythm of his heartbeat, the soothing sound of his voice, but not the words. I had heard what my heart needed to hear. Here was someone who loved me and saw me, not as a woman who needed improvement, but as a person worthy of love, just as I was.

The next morning, I said, "Sorry I fell asleep while you were talking."

"You heard everything I wanted you to know," he said gently.

By December, I gave him a key to my apartment. It was a big deal for me. I had never lived with a man since my divorce or integrated one into my life with my sons. But David was not like anyone I had ever met. This relationship felt solid and brought with it the devotion that I had dreamt of as a young woman. And by speaking words with intention and then living them day by day, we gradually built a life that was a home within our hearts and minds, together.

Three years later, we decided that marriage, although a scary word for each of us, was the right choice. We had already committed to one another. Marriage became the natural next step. I made him promise that I would die in his arms. He agreed.

We said our vows on a sand dune near our apartment, promising honesty, patience and committing to helping one another grow as human beings in this crazy-assed life, embracing the beloved. Three weeks later in a friend's garden, we did so again before a minister in front of family and friends.

What stretched out before us now was a life where we touched every day, where we didn't go to bed angry, and where coffee and guitars were the norm at the kitchen table on weekend mornings. We called it the Church of Dave. I played and sang while he leaned into the spaces in my songs, where the sound of his guitar and mine blended together, just as our love and life did. Sometimes a tug here was an invitation to follow. Sometimes a push there was an invitation to lead. Music and love are unique in that way. We harmonized and created something new in a delicate dance as we played together. We did that for many years. And just like the music we made, we ebbed and flowed as individuals and as a couple. Gibran spoke of the need for space between lovers, for only then can love grow in that space. Every so often, we would catch each other's gaze and fall in love again. It delighted us both that ten years, twenty years, almost thirty years later, we could still find that feeling of discovery.

No one belongs to anyone forever. We are on loan, I suppose. One spring evening, after a day that started with music and coffee, and ended with holding each other in bed, he began having chest pains. As I drove him to the emergency room, he broke his promise to me. He sighed out of this physical life and into whatever awaits us. As someone who had been a hospice nurse, David wanted no one to fight Death for his body. However, I never even had the chance to go to battle.

Soulmates. We were that. Willing to take the risk that our hearts might be broken again and yet unable to turn away. Our hearts and souls strained toward each other.

There is a fine line between vulnerability and availability. Yet, nothing real can come into your life if you don't hold both within your bones. We must be willing to gamble on love.

I would never have known him if I had not been willing to surrender into the unknown, and my life would be less as a result. Now I'm surrendering into my life as it unfolds without his physical presence. The love, though, goes on and on. Always.

***

Patti Shaffner is a singer/songwriter, actress, director, performance coach, improv singer, and most recently, a storyteller and writer. Her songwriting has garnered local and national awards, and her acting and directing have been recognized for excellence by Northwest Indiana Excellence in Theater Foundation (NIETF).

Patti has been performing professionally for over thirty years and has found, through many avenues, that art, music, and storytelling are the glue that binds us all together and gives meaning and beauty to our lives. She believes it is the responsibility of the artist to give voice to what otherwise might go unexpressed.

Though life is quite different without her beloved David, she delights in her three sons and their families, and many friends. Patti lives on the southernmost shore of Lake Michigan, in Indiana, a few minutes' walk from the water.

Her website is: jazzdakini.com

Chapter 14 | Lucy Love by Tonya L. Clanton

I didn't use to feel apathetic about dogs; I loathed them. "You don't like *dogs*?" People would say with a look that suggested I was a callous hater of all purely good things: puppies, Christmas, and rainbows. But the fact was that I heartily disliked dogs because they were so needy. Cats were like middle schoolers, whose elusive acceptance I respected, whereas dogs were like kindergartners, who frightened me with their intensity and eternally sticky hands. I spotted the slimy drool-makers across the room and walked the other way. I chided my mother for caving into her husband's request to get a dog.

"Dogs are so much work," I told her. If I wanted something that messy in my house, I might as well adopt a drunk toddler.

What I wanted was a baby of my own. I was ready for all of *that* mess, the eight loads of laundry a day, the spit-up, the crying. I was confident I'd be the mother of my dreams. We tried. We signed up for the shots—giant needles that made my butt bruised and lumpy. I gripped the doorframe with my pants around my ankles, bit into a washcloth, and trusted my husband along with modern science to inject baby-making drugs into my body.

Four years of ovulation calendars and doctor visits, staring at the successful baby photo wall grinning down at me. Four years of avoiding alcohol, except when I couldn't take it anymore—when I had to crumple in the bathtub and console myself with whiskey, when it didn't work the first time, and the second time when my ovaries swelled to the size of softballs due to the overstimulation. Four failed IVF attempts in four years, and finally we called it quits. Four years later, I nearly died when one of my overworked ovaries turned on itself with infection. I had to have it removed, and my mom flew out to stitch me back together. I was forty, with one ovary and a debilitating reservoir of hope. Four weeks after my surgery, we were shopping for, I kid-you-not, cat furniture, and happened to walk past the animal shelter.

"Oh, you've got to look at the dogs," my mom said as she dragged me by the hand.

The entire room was one big, continuous bark fest. I walked in with my hands over my ears, and my eyes immediately locked with the only animal in the place *not* going crazy. A jet-black shepherd dog with a white tuxedo-shirt chest sat back on her haunches, alone in her cage, looking as if her party invitation was lost in the mail. Her ears folded back, she sat silently absorbing the sadness of the room as if she was resigned to the misery. She stared right through me, and her velvet triangle ears perked up with hope.

"Cuss, that's my dog." And then I saw her nametag: Lucy. That was the name I envisioned for our little girl. She was a person who I never got to meet. I texted her picture to my husband.

In two seconds, his response was, "Get her."

I love her with the fierceness of a teenage girl at a Taylor Swift concert. It's platonic, but it's magical. It's like I can see an eighty-year-old woman's eyes in hers, with all the wisdom and understanding I saw in my grandmother. She gets me out of the house daily, she greets me with unabashed enthusiasm. The weight of her bulky body leaning against me on the couch feels like what I imagined a sturdy four-year-old to feel like, tuckered out after a day of jumping on trampolines and collecting fireflies.

Sometimes my grief feels nebulous—unreachable, like the struggle I felt the first time I tried to dial an iPhone, like trying to dial a cat. Like a cloud that hangs so low for a second, pressing down on you with all its might, and then suddenly lifts just out of reach. Like how grief is *supposed* to feel?

And Lucy makes me feel better at these moments. She is mending me.

Sometimes when I look at her, I think, *We saved you from that cold cement cage, but you saved us too.* She was seven and a half when we adopted her, and the volunteer who cared for her said Lucy cried for two weeks straight after being dumped there by her former owners. No one paid attention to her because they were all intent on finding the perfect small puppy, fresh, with no backstory.

Lucy loves us, and we love her. She has stamped our family with a capital "L" like one of those cute signet rings. When we're together, I have a purpose. I am here to love this dog—me—the person who professed her disgust at this species her whole adult life. I didn't know how full my heart could feel from one special animal. All she wants all day long is to be with us, to lick our hands, go on ridiculously long hikes, and snuggle on the couch. In the woods, she is well-behaved enough to be off leash. She runs ahead about twenty feet, testing her freedom, and looks back at every corner. If I cry out from tripping on a root or need help crossing a creek, she is there. Every night, she sleeps between us like a warm log.

Her love and dependence transformed me. Owning a dog makes me responsible for a life. I can't stay inside all weekend crying through *This is Us* or re-watching *Parenthood* for the thousandth time. I have to get out and show her the world, so *both* of us can be healthy. I feel a connection with her that is visceral. We have a symbiotic relationship. This nearly twelve-year-old puppy is as old as my grief, but she is stronger than it as well. I am so grateful that we found each other. And if life had worked out the way I planned, I wouldn't have changed from a cold-blooded puppy-hater to a fiercely loyal mom with a furry baby.

***

Tonya L. Clanton is a writer and educator who is transitioning from a fifteen-year career as a teacher to life as a full-time writer. She has interviewed social activists and artists, written travel essays for online publications, and published a personal narrative, *Babies, Business, Books* on ourlifelogs.com. She shared her writing on community radio station, Asheville FM, as DJ TLC, in her show, *Sunday Splendor*, where she curated themed playlists and mixed in positive news stories. This story is her first piece to be published in a book, and she is excited to join this talented group of storytellers. Originally from Illinois, she now lives in Asheville, North Carolina with her husband and their dog, Lucy. She enjoys exploring used bookstores, hiking with her family, and learning all she can about the people and stories that create our shared history.

Chapter 15 | The Hockey Helmet by Randy Richardson

My little sister can't stop crying, and it annoys the hell out of me. *Grow up*, I want to tell her. But I don't say a word. No one in this family says anything.

The house feels empty now that my dad's living ten miles away. I act like it's no big deal because that's what a big brother is supposed to do. Ten years old and I'm the man of the family. I don't want this. I didn't ask for this. I want to just be a kid again.

The house is too quiet when I close my bedroom door at night. That's when the tears I've stored up all day come pouring out onto the pillow and the sleeves of my Chicago Bears pajamas. This family tension has been going on for a week now. I want it to stop. I want my dad back home where he belongs.

My mom is still here, but she's not the same mom. With an extra button opened on her blouse and her skin-tight flare jeans, my mom doesn't look like the other moms. I'm certain that it's the women's lib group she's going to that's responsible for her transformation. I want my old mom back, the one who was always there for me—not the one who leaves us home with a babysitter I can't stand, so that she can work as a hostess at that new Italian restaurant on the corner.

My eight-year-old sister and I sit at the dinner table picking at the chop suey from a can. My mom looks like she's on the verge of tears, and I blame her, and then I don't.

"We're going for a drive," she says.

In the backseat of the Maverick, my sister looks to me. She is confused. I shrug, holding back the urge to slug her. I know she's hurting.

But can't she see I'm hurting too? I just want her to leave me alone. Because I know what she's thinking, and I can't stop thinking the same thing: *What did we do wrong?* Really, the question that plagues me is: *What did I do wrong?* Because I can't stop blaming myself for what has happened. Was it because I wet the bed? Or was it that day I pulled the cord on the record player and the flames started?

I've no idea where we're going, but I don't care as I look out the window at the glowing streetlights and neon signs on the storefronts, which are a welcome sight only because they aren't the four walls of my bedroom.

Twenty minutes later, we're in the near-empty parking lot of Children's Bargain Town. My mom cranes her neck to look at us sitting in a rare state of calm in the backseat, as far away from one another as we can be, yet somehow closer than we've ever been. "You each get to pick out one toy," she tells us.

Our heads turn simultaneously, and from the two ends of the back seat, tentative eyes meet. Turning to my mom, I broach the question that I'm sure my sister won't ask but is dying to know, "Any toy?"

"Well," she says, "within reason."

What the hell does that mean? Five dollars? Ten? Twenty? Does it mean as big as a basketball, but not as big as a bicycle? The various calculations are running through my head like a stock ticker, and I realize that for the first time since my parents sat us down a week ago and broke the news to us they were splitting, I wasn't thinking about that one word that I couldn't bring myself to say to anyone.

Divorce. Such a cold word. I zip my jacket all the way to the neck to protect against the chill in the air.

You hear things on the playground. Hurtful things. Kids say things without even thinking, oftentimes without even knowing what they're saying. I've heard them talk about broken families. I didn't know any families that were broken. I didn't know you could break a family; that your mom and dad could just call it quits and that suddenly you could have two houses and not just one.

Why instead of running out of the house and crying, didn't I make them stop yelling at each other? *Stop! Stop! Stop! What are you doing? Why are you hurting each other? Why are you hurting me?*

***

The store is enormous. I glance at my mom, and she gives me the nod. I wander through the aisles filled with GI Joe action figures and Rock 'Em Sock 'Em Robots. It feels like Christmas in July.

I am overwhelmed by it all, both literally and figuratively. Too many choices. Too many uncertainties. It's not just the toys. It's my life. The life that I knew. The life I liked. The life I *loved*. I'm paralyzed by the uncertainty of what my life will be like now. As I take in all the toys that surround me, I realize there is no toy in this gigantic store that will change this plain and simple fact: that I am now nobody, that what I really want is a time machine—a toy that will make things right again and put my dad back in the house and stop my sister from crying, and dry all the wetness off my pillowcase and pajama sleeves.

When I get to the checkout line, I see my sister tightly holding a doll. I hand my mom a ten-dollar hockey helmet. It's like the one that Stan Mikita wears, only it's not, because his is white and this one is blue. My mom hesitates as her brows furrow. "This is your choice?" I nod, understanding her confusion.

I don't play hockey, except for the table-top game that is made for two people but which I play by myself. Pretending to be Mikita, I win the face-off and then chase down the puck in the corner. Spinning around, I take the slap shot. Because I maneuver all the players with their levers, that means I'm the goalie, too. Of course, I can't get to the lever on the other side of the rink in time to stop the puck from going into the net.

The truth is, I can barely stand on ice skates. My mom knows this.

In the backseat of the Maverick, I rip the tags off the helmet as my mom starts up the car. I place the helmet on my head. It fits snugly; warm, like a blanket, but hard, like a protective shell. In the rearview, I catch my mom's eyes and read the worry on them. In return, I offer a slight smile. Can she see how much I love her? Can she see how much I needed this helmet? Can she see that I'm going to be okay?

****

An attorney and award-winning journalist, **Randy Richardson** is a founding member and first president of the nonprofit Chicago Writers Association. He is the first male recipient of the National Federation of Press Women's Communicator of Achievement Award and was named to *NewCity*'s *2019* "Lit 50: Who Really Books in Chicago" list. His essays have been published in the anthologies *Chicken Soup for the Father and Son Soul, Humor for a Boomer's Heart, The Big Book of Christmas Joy*, and *Cubbie Blues: 100 Years of Waiting Till Next Year*, as well as in numerous print and online journals. He is the author of two novels, *Cheeseland* and *Lost in the Ivy*, and coauthor of *Cubsessions: Famous Fans of Chicago's North Side Baseball Team,* all from Eckhartz Press. You can learn more about Randy by visiting his website, randyrichardson.co

Chapter 16 | Brakes/Breaks by Barrie Cole

I've fallen in love again. I've slammed into love and here it is, the whole parade of it with its cymbals and bugles and drums, and all its ceaseless marching on the heart. Here is love with its muddy footprints and wet grasses.

Love is like some kind of baby; hungry, beautiful, demanding of everything. Or perhaps, instead, love is more like an accident, only sexier. The truth is, whatever it is, when love happens, the happening of love, I say, "Okay, I'm in." I mean really, who am I to say no to the dense, flourless chocolate cake of the thing? Who are any of us to say no? Unexpected love feels like a new room with extra, open windows, and so it's important to bear the pleasure of the breezes and the sunlight spilling and spilling itself all over the floors.

He and I begin as friends and then it is as if a little Japanese walking bridge appears, and we are invited to cross it. At the time, we are both dating terrible people; manipulative, abusive, non-grown—upy people; people with whom we find sex astonishing, mind-blowing, truly incredible. But the problem is that some very necessary and interesting parts of ourselves are out to lunch and never quite return from the hotdog stand. This is troublesome, not only to us, but to our friends and therapists and co-workers. We suffer. We complain. We make declarations to leave. We have astonishingly amazing sex again with the horrible people who are good at sex, *again.*

We change our minds. We make up excuses.

And then...

Somewhere along the timeline of lattes, Earl Grey, and cheap Vietnamese noodles, (which often only one of us drinks or eats because the other one is too sad or strung out), we realize something big. Instead of pining over these people who are not good for us, maybe we could be with each other! And the bridge that appears, seems sturdy and easy, there is nothing tightrope-y about it. And even better, the bridge is pretty, like a bridge in a Monet painting. The colors of the bridge smudge together and cover us, and we walk around inside all the colors.

I cross the bridge immediately. There is a little fall-out, but mostly I just feel relief. Each day I feel less like a ghost and more whole, opaque. I am able to make my children breakfasts involving pans and eggs instead of handing each of them a granola bar. My ex-lover tries to seduce me back, but I hold out. Suddenly, I don't even see what I saw in her, and I think how easy it is to make things up. Wow, I say to myself, I turned a junkyard into a tropical rainforest in my mind, and it wasn't until all the junkyard dogs began barking and rattling their chains that it occurred to me that dogs with spiked collars and menacing incisors are not butterflies.

Okay, I'm simplifying a bit. There were some dramatic moments and some heroin-like withdrawal feelings, along with some self-condemnation for being in the former relationship to begin with, but this didn't last too long. I was in pretty good shape. The hexagons and trapezoids and quadrangles of me looked no worse for the wear, which was no small thing considering I'd barely passed geometry in high school.

But unlike me, he only sort of crosses the bridge, which is not *actually* crossing, and the purpose of a bridge is mostly for crossing, not standing there. And just standing there was exactly what he was doing.

"Um, hello?" I ask, "I'm on this side. What are you doing?"

"I don't know," he yells back. "I feel guilty."

"What? Why would you feel guilty? She's horrible. We've done nothing but talk about how horrible she is for months!"

"I know," he admits.

"How come you're not walking over here?" I yell. "You have legs, right? You have feet, right?"

"My feet are stuck," he yells back. "I have my brakes on, like on a car."

"That sucks," I yell back. "Because I think I might really love you."

"I absolutely know I love you," he yells. "I'm positive we were meant for each other."

"Okay. Could you maybe try to wiggle something or accelerate? By the way, I'm speaking metaphorically!"

"I know you are. I get it! I'm too afraid. I just can't!"

He stays on the bridge. I stay on the other side.

We send beautiful love letters through the modern networks, and the letters pop up on screens. These letters are traditionally called emails, of course, but *love emails* doesn't sound very romantic at all, and these emails were very much so.

He writes, "You know what? You smell like a kitten. You're irresistible."

I respond, "You smell like cinnamon toast. You zig zag through me."

Despite his brakes, there are many make-out sessions in my car. He doesn't have a car, just a bicycle. If he wasn't stuck on the bridge, I am sure we would make out on his bicycle too, if that were possible. In fact, if he wasn't stuck, we could probably make out on, near, in front of, and behind his bicycle. We could try all the make-out positions regarding his bicycle. But he won't leave her. He won't cross the bridge.

I say, "So I've been thinking about these brakes you have. I know a good mechanic. Do you want me to see if he can rip them out?"

"I think I'm close," he says.

"I'm coming to the end of my rope," I finally say. "So much so, that there's really no rope left at all. I'm holding onto well… nothing. Air is hard to grasp onto. If the brakes stay, I'm going to have to take a break from you… from us."

"I don't want you to do that," he says.

"I don't either," I say.

"Let's go back to being friends for a while," he suggests.

We try that. We end up making out in my car again, in the cemetery. The warmth and tenderness between us is so electrifying that a coyote creeps out of the woods to see us. Even the dead seem slightly less dead.

I want to demolish his brakes, and then I want to demolish him with love. I want him to test-drive that for a change. He's so stuck. I'm so stupid. How could I be in this? I feel a kind of otherness in my position. I can't locate myself. It feels awful to wait perpetually to become real. *Do I like this? What is this?*

In order to cope, I make a decision that I will Walt Whitman my life. That is my plan. I decide to make Nature my lover with a capital N. It is spring, after all, and the trees in the park speak to me of new life. I don't care how much of a cliche it is. The icicles drip and shine, the sheet cakes of snow on the picnic tables melt and disappear. I am mostly happy, I try to stay away from him, but he won't stop emailing and texting. So I write back, "If you won't cross the bridge, if you really can't do it, please, please, leave me alone."

It is so hard for me to say that.

He tells me it is hard for him to read it too.

One night I can't sleep and take a night-time walk at one in the morning. The moon is exquisite and full, and there is an aura of haziness around her too. She is like someone telling a scary story with a flashlight under her chin. I walk the path through the park and wish the moon would release a permission slip. If such a thing existed, I imagine it would twirl down, and that the slip would have his name on it. I would pick it up and give it to him and say, "The moon gave me this permission slip, and it has your name on it, so guess what? I think you can leave her now. We can be together."

And then I think how wonderful it is that permission sounds so much like persimmon, and there is a kind of beauty and pleasure in that. Language can do things for people even when other people can't do anything at all: can't move, or leave, or follow through. I feel an appreciation for the reliability, the dependability of language.

And although I'm unable to give him permission for us, I *can* give him persimmons, and that is something. Persimmons are close to permissions, at least in spelling, and so they could represent hope, or possibility, or just something sweet to cling to.

I go to a few different special grocery stores to find persimmons. I bring my kids with me. It's a persimmon hunt. At the Korean market we stare at enormous crabs in tanks. They want to buy one and keep it as a pet. I tell them, "No." They wave goodbye to it.

They say, "Bye Mr. Crab, bye Mister Crabby Crab."

I buy them lime candy instead. In the car they make up a song:

"We didn't get a crab

But we got candy.

It's green!"

The "*It's green*" line is especially enjoyable. They roll down the windows and sing that particular line louder and louder and crack themselves up. They demand I turn around at the stoplight to view their green tongues.

At the third store, I locate some persimmons in a little cardboard box with blue writing. The persimmons are orange and blimp shaped. I leave them at his door with a note about the permissions I wish he would give himself, and persimmons, which he now has. He writes me again, "I love you so much."

"I love you so much." *What does that even mean,* I wonder. *He loves me so much?* I change the words around in my mind, playing with the syntax.

I love you so much
I much you love so
So much love
Love so much so
Much much love I
Love so much you
I love much much
So much you love I
So much I love you
You love so much
So much so love I so
And it goes on and on like that…

***

Barrie Cole is a Chicago-based writer, playwright, essayist, poet, and performer. Some of her plays include *Reverse Gossip, Elevator Tours, Clumsy Sublime, Fruit Tree Backpack, and Reality is an Activity*. Critic, Justin Hayford of the Chicago Reader has written, "Her ambiguously concrete work layers childlike simplicity over seasoned melancholy to produce piercing, wondrous images of charming, discomfiting transformation." Most recently, she has been working on a series of run-on sentence poems as well as a collection of essays about language tentatively titled: *Control Issues*. To learn more about Barrie and read more of her work, please visit http://www.barriecole.com

Chapter 17 | Nothing You Can Do about It by Paul Teodo and Tom Myers

She reached out to me. She was blind, mostly deaf too. She struggled to locate my face, gently grasping it with her bony purple fingers as she said, "I love you, and there is nothing you can do about it." She was 103. She said she was praying for me because the last time I visited, I looked troubled. Stillness consumed us; I felt a deep warmth coming from a place that seemed foreign to me.

I met her eight years ago when I worked in West Englewood. It was a poor people's hospital on Chicago's South Side. I'd been canned from a prestigious medical center in the western suburbs, inhabited by a staff and clientele with no clue this *poor people's hospital* even existed. She was a lot younger then, just ninety-five. At that time, she was pushing around a walker adorned with fluffy stuffed animals, red streamers, and reading a book a week. She pulled on my sleeve and said, "You have intense eyes, I bet you're a good listener!"

Sister Lorianna entered this world in 1915. Born in the middle of a pack of thirteen children. From the *old country*, Lithuania, an ancient land, once the largest in Europe. It had been around over a thousand years. It first declared independence in 1253, again after WWI, and again in 1990. The Russians finally vacated the Republic in 1993. The Final Solution began there. During the Nazi occupation, 195,000 of its 200,000 Jews were exterminated.

Her family immigrated in 1921. She was raised near the Pennsylvania coal mines. Ordained in 1934, she was sent to work as a teacher in Hispanic and African American schools on Chicago's South Side and later became a hospital chaplain before retiring in 1985.

On a cold Saturday afternoon in February, I visited her after rounds at the hospital. I rang the doorbell to the Motherhouse where she and the other nuns lived. One of them led me to a small sitting room where Sister Lorianna sat, a lone candle twinkled in the dim light. We talked about life, death, God, pain, and friendship. A peace came over me in the stillness and shadows.

"Sister," I said.

She grasped my hand and smiled, "yes?"

"Sitting here with you is like taking really good drugs."

An impish grin graced her face. "I think you like me."

"Sister," I said, "you're a mystic. I bet you could levitate right off that walker and fly around."

Her sightless eyes seemed to scan the walls of the sitting room as if preparing herself for flight. She took a deep breath as she considered it, "I've never tried."

She was my friend. My good friend. The last time I visited her, I said a prayer out loud. I asked, "Sister, how'd I do?" I made the prayer up off the top of my head. She gave me a thumbs up, then said in her soft raspy voice, "A+!"

First A+ I ever got from a nun.

She told me, "I talked to Mother Superior and a priest."

I didn't understand.

She could tell. "It's okay now, I have permission. They no longer give me medicine, take my blood pressure, draw blood, run tests, or give me solid food.

She continued, "It's my time."

She wasn't sad or depressed. She looked relieved.

She asked if I wanted to hear a joke. She always had a half dozen or so ready when I visited. Usually the same ones. I said, "Sure."

She smiled. "Two boys loved baseball. One of them said to the other, 'Do you think there is baseball in heaven?' The one boy said, 'I'm not sure, I hope so. If I get there before you, I'll let you know.' The boy dies. He comes back to his friend and says, 'Good News! There is baseball in heaven, *and you're pitching tomorrow*!'" She howled with laughter, struggling through the punch line.

We both fell silent.

"Sister."

"Yes?" she leaned towards me, her wrinkled face serious, but full of curiosity.

"Can I ask you a favor?"

"Anything."

"Come back and tell me when I'm pitching!"

She cackled with joy and smacked my arm. She loved it, and I loved that she loved it.

I kissed her goodbye. In her diminished but firm voice, she pointed her twisted purple finger at me, "I love you Buster, and there's nothing you can do about it."

On October 19, 2019, at the height of the Covid pandemic, Sister Lorianna passed. She was 107. On the same day, we published our second book, *Call Me Z*. One of the main characters in the book, a wizened nun with unshakeable faith, was patterned after Sister Lorianna.

I loved her… and there was nothing she could do about it.

***

Tom Myers is a retired Navy Commander who served at sea in numerous ships and in Iraq with the Multi-National Force.

Paul Teodo is a retired health-care executive who specialized in turning around inner-city hospitals. He is a noted award-winning Chicago storyteller, recognized nationally. They have co-authored two novels, *Pastaman* and *Call Me Z*.

Chapter 18 | For Love of the Museum by Jill Howe

It wasn't the most obvious choice to fall in love with a gorilla. It all started when I was a child. I felt most at ease in the Field Museum. The echoes of shoes in the massive Stanley Hall, the great totem poles of the Pacific Northwest that have towered for decades, and the slightly sweet aroma of wax melting from the machines that make wax dinosaurs, would fill my senses with a word: home. I would go several times a year with my parents. When I turned fourteen, I was allowed to take the Metra train by myself to the museum. The only directions for the city I needed were to exit at Union Station, turn right, hit the lake, turn right, and head to the white marble steps of the Field Museum. History oozes from every marble column. I would bring my charcoal and pastels, so I could draw the taxidermized animals in the Hall of Mammals.

On one visit, I explored the bowels of the museum. In a dusty corner next to an enormous red granite sarcophagus, I found him. There is no king more noble and powerful than the lowland gorilla. The wood panel underneath his giant regal head said, "Bushman," and a copper cast of his hand was displayed. I placed my hand in his, as he seemed to look forever, slightly away from me. Perhaps it was that coyness that led me back to draw Bushman again and again. The curve of his back, the bulk of his arms, the curled knuckles, the stolid and mysterious glint in his eyes as he looked into a distance that didn't exist. More than once, I thought I saw him move, but perhaps that was a child's fancy. He stared out at a small, dark corner of the basement under a dirty yellow fluorescent light. It was like finding a king in a fairy tale, trapped in ice.

Thirty years later, I was asked, as a professional storyteller, to tell stories to the kids who spend the night at the museums for their program, Dozin' with the Dinos. I always wondered how I could get a staff ID for the Field because I had looked at job postings every year and wasn't qualified for any. This was one of the strangest ways to get admittance and felt like a lie–a giant fluke someone would catch at any moment. Something deep inside me stirred. I felt a pull when I was asked which exhibit I wanted to tell stories about. Out of the pages of my sketchbook emerged Bushman's stoic face.

Unfortunately, the museum staff told me his dusty corner wasn't big enough for the kids to sit for a story hour. "You can tell it down the hall by his photo," they explained. It was certainly a beautiful photograph, at least six by eight feet tall. I knew not to argue, but Bushman wanted attention. I could feel it. I knew nothing about him because his plaque only read, "Bushman."

I started my research immediately. I learned that in 1928, Bushman was found as an orphan in the jungles of Cameroon and suckled by an ambiguous "native woman" until he was two years old. In truth, they ripped him from his gorilla mother's arms like so many other gorillas who were taken, and who subsequently died during their journey across the sea from West Africa to America. Their eventual destinations were circuses and zoos who paid hefty prices for them. The first to make it across the Atlantic would be the only gorilla in North America.

Bushman's poacher was crafty and not willing to lose his fee, so he left the young gorilla with a missionary family, the Smiths, for a few years until he was strong enough to make the journey. Winifred Smith, Bushman's first love, was only a child when Bushman became a part of her family. She treated him as a brother, and they played together every day as Bushman was allowed the same access to the house as the children. When Bushman was two, Winifred lost her sibling because the poacher sold him to Lincoln Park Zoo in 1930. The zoo paid $3,500 for him.

When Bushman arrived at Lincoln Park Zoo, he was a total celebrity. King Kong fever had kids and adults alike bringing their favorite bad guy to life. Everyone ultimately fell in love with him because he was a magnificent goofball. He would stand for nothing less than being the center of attention. Eddie Robinson, Bushman's lifelong zookeeper, wrestled and played football with him until Bushman was a teen. Although Bushman grew into a massive 550 pounds, he still wanted to play. He didn't understand how strong he had become. When he turned his seventy-five-foot lead rope into a giant tug-of-war, he violently pulled Eddie, his zookeeper and friend, down the stairs. After that, they forever left him to play on his own in a bare concrete cage with thick bars.

What he loved most was the children who came to visit, swinging from his tire, the one allegedly from Hitler's car, a gift from the USO for boosting morale among the soldiers. Time magazine gave him the title: Best Known and Popular Civic Figure in Chicago. Every year on his birthday, thousands of school children came to visit and brought him dozens of bread and vegetable birthday cakes with celery candles on top. They sang 'Happy Birthday' to him at the top of their lungs. He loved throwing cake at the photographers as the children laughed hysterically.

But life in a bare concrete cage was boring and small. One day, Eddie forgot to lock the cage, and he escaped to the kitchen where he ate everything he could find and then refused to get back into his cage. The zookeepers used a garter snake to get him back in his cage. Apparently, the King of the Jungle turned into a little baby around snakes. Shenanigans continued until 1953. But sadly, at the age of twenty-three, Bushman passed away from a massive heart attack. Thousands of people lined up at Lincoln Park Zoo to pay tribute. On New Year's Day he was gone. Children looked into his empty cage for months after, sure that nothing could ever replace this amazing creature they considered a friend.

As I collected photos, scoured online newspaper archives, read an eBook version of an old tome about the beginning days of Lincoln Park Zoo, it all painted the soul of a unique creature. A personality that could be both awe-inspiring and silly, jealous, and sweet. I saw him as a pioneer of sorts, going first in a long line of primates that stretch until now at the

Zoo's Regenstein Center for African Apes. The experts of the day said Bushman lived to a ripe old age of twenty-three based on their limited knowledge of the lifespan of a lowland gorilla. In the wild, a lowland gorilla should live to be about thirty-five to forty-years old.

The impact he made on people was tremendous. Winifred Smith, Bushman's human sister, never forgot her childhood with him. Bushman loved his humans and insisted on being carried everywhere. It was not surprising that when Winifred was ninety-two, she felt an urge to see Bushman one last time before she died. Several newspapers and magazines captured pictures of her reunion with Bushman. What was she thinking as she looked at her grown playmate? What memories of joy did she recall from her childhood? Was she sad to see him in a small cage? Winifred was indeed a kindred spirit. As I learned about her, I felt her nudging me forward to continue to learn more about Bushman, her sweet and silly brother.

At this point in my research, something unusual happened; Bushman communicated with me. I didn't hear his voice but felt an energy that took me deeper into his life, behind the zoo's shiny facade. The biggest tragedy I sensed was that Bushman was alone. Bushman hated being alone. Other zoos around the country wouldn't let their female gorillas mate with Bushman because they felt the females were in jeopardy because of Bushman's massive strength. A gorilla was too valuable an asset for a zoo to lose. I proceeded with my story in front of his large photo because I wasn't allowed to tell it in front of him. However, I felt as if he was saying to me, "I got this."

A few weeks later, the Field Museum emailed and said there were plans to move Bushman over to where his portrait was prominently displayed in the East hallway. My museum colleagues looked at me like I was a witch. I felt Bushman give me a wink. They not only moved Bushman but also made a new digital interface with all kinds of stories about him. He was dusty too, so they vacuumed him. He looked like a man with a new satin suit. So handsome!

I was excited, and I felt Bushman was too. I knew what he missed the most: kids on his birthday. One fib I say each time I tell his story is that *today* is Bushman's birthday. I see it as making up for the decades of missed birthdays. After I share everything I love about Bushman, I have the kids bring their flashlights up to the exhibit and shine their lights on him. I turn off all the lights in the hall, grab my ukulele, and we sing Happy Birthday to Bushman while their flashlights light him up in the dark hall. At the end of the song, they point their flashlights toward the ceiling, like so many candles, and we all "blow them out" by turning off all the flashlights at once. More than one child bears witness to seeing Bushman move, as I always did as a child. In that dark silence when the flashlights go out, I have heard a "Thank you," from him. It's like a huge hug. As the children come up to me after, some want more information because they're curious. And museum kids really are the best. Bushman will take any extra attention he can receive.

After I say goodbye to the last pajama-clad-museum nerd, I take off my mic and turn off the sound system. I get all packed up in the dark with Bushman. Did I see his eyes move? By that time, it's almost midnight. I am there totally alone with him in museum darkness, which is an abnormal and completely different kind of darkness. So much history in one place, multiple floors of offices and archives hidden from public view and a basement of specimens that seem to go on for miles. I can imagine Bushman wanting to get out of his case. Keeping history alive is paying tribute to those who got us to where we are now. I'm not the first or the last person to say, there is magic at the museum… if you listen carefully.

***

Jill Howe is the producer of *Story Sessions* since 2013, a curated showcase featuring true stories and real-time illustrations at Golden Dagger in Lincoln Park. *Story Sessions* also has a monthly open mic for storytellers at Sauce & Bread Kitchen in Edgewater. Jill has facilitated her monthly storytelling group, *Friends with Words*, for the last nine years. She organizes and teaches *Story Sessions* writing retreats, and she has presented a Tedx Talk on vulnerability through storytelling. Jill is also the resident storytelling instructor at Chicago's historic Newberry Library. She shares her stories at bars and theaters all around Chicagoland. Her work is featured in *Tomorrow's Storytellers Today* (Parkhurst Publishing, 2021) and *Chicago Storytellers From Stage to Page* (Chicago Story Press, 2020).

Chapter 19 | The Ocean by Anne E. Beall

Love is like a body of water. In my teens and early adulthood, it seemed like an ocean that forcefully splashed me and then retreated. I relished the spray and the salt, which were exhilarating, but then I felt cold and uncomfortable. After the first waves receded, I would stand at the shore and shiver as the sun went down.

After I fell in love the first time, that feeling was the barometer I used to measure my relationships; I looked for the kind of longing that would knock me off my feet and make it difficult to concentrate. It was like an alcoholic beverage that was powerful and sweet in the beginning, although it grew sour over the course of the night. Love, I thought, had equal parts of longing and rejection.

When I met Michael, it didn't feel like an ocean wave hitting me squarely in the face. Our first date was at a local bar, and I enjoyed our conversation. He seemed familiar, almost as if I'd met him before. We weren't at the seaside but rather sitting by a small pond. I thought we might go for a swim.

That night we drank beer, ate fish and chips, and went for a walk by Lake Michigan. We talked about many things. He was attentive when I spoke, but he was also interesting. Our date stretched out in time without our realizing it was going on for several hours. And then we ran into my ex-husband. There is nothing that will ruin a first date faster than a head-on collision with an ex-spouse from a bitter divorce. The spouse and the divorce devastated me emotionally and financially.

My thoughts shattered and spilt out in nonsensical phrases.

"Um, we need to turn around. We have to go another way."

Michael looked at me quizzically.

"My ex-husband is over there, and I don't want to—"

"That's fine."

We turned and walked in the other direction. I tried to remember what we were talking about and spoke quickly. Michael was silent.

And then he put his arm around me and said, "Are you okay?"

My mind was storming, and he had extended an umbrella over my head. The hail wasn't hitting me. The clouds would pass, and I'd be dry.

"I'm fine. Thanks for asking."

When we said goodbye that night, he kissed me the way men kiss women in the movies. I didn't expect it. I thought, *I'll have to consider a swim in that pond.*

After we dated for a few months, he made dinner at his house, and I met his two teenage sons. We began heading out on long walks, talking for hours. That feeling of being splashed and knocked over never happened. But something else did. I waded into that pond without realizing it, and one day I looked down and I wasn't standing at the edge anymore. I was in the water. And he was there next to me. The water wasn't too cold. It was serene.

We spent more time together and even went on a vacation. Weekends without him seemed long, and weekends with him seemed short. I shared my writing with him, and he shared his research articles with me. We sought each other's opinions on topics great and small.

One afternoon, I received a call that they had taken my mother to an Intensive Care Unit in Maine. She was mumbling odd phrases. My stepsister, who is a nurse, suggested I come to Maine immediately because my mother might die. I dissolved into tears on Michael's shoulder. He comforted me and offered to take me to the airport, look after my cat, and do anything else I needed.

There was a silence as I tried to process everything.

"I love you," I said to him.

"I love you too," he replied.

I glanced down and saw that I was no longer knee-deep in water. I was up to my shoulders. It felt good.

One night after I got back, we went out to a club with friends. Michael and I danced all night long. He requested several songs and danced toward me with a big smile. I felt light and free.

"I think you should marry me," I said.

"I think I should too."

When I looked down this time, I realized I wasn't in a pond at all. It was a lake, a large one, with a beautiful sunset and I wasn't just standing there, waiting for the waves to hit. I was treading water. The lake was the right temperature. He was nearby, and it was sublime.

Several months later, Michael and I went to our favorite bar, the one where we had our first date. We had returned from a weekend away, and neither of us felt like cooking. After our waitress served us with beers, he got down on one knee and asked me to marry him.

Now I saw I was in an immense body of water, and we were nowhere near the shore. We were both swimming. I alternated between floating on top and diving underneath. This was neither a pond nor a lake. This was an ocean, as big and as wide as I could imagine. I realized then that I'd never actually been out this far in any body of water. I'd never even been in the ocean before. All those times the waves had hit, I'd been on the shore getting splashed by the tide. I had experienced the excitement of getting wet, but the water never actually held me. I knew there would be waves; when you immerse yourself in water, there are always waves. But these would be different. These would be waves we would traverse together.

"Yes, I'll marry you," I said, with tears in my eyes.

***

Anne E. Beall, PhD, is a writer and storyteller who has published ten books on a variety of topics. She has been interviewed on NPR about her book, *Heroic, Helpful & Caring Cats*, and her book *Cinderella Didn't Live Happily Ever After* was featured in People Magazine.

Her other books include: *5-Minute Sleep Meditations: Fantasy Journeys with an Inspirational Message*; *5-Minute Meditation Vacations: Magical Journeys with a Personal Message*; *Community Cats: A Journey into the World of Feral Cats; Heartfelt Connections: How Animals and People Help One Another; Reading the Hidden Communications Around You: A Guide to Reading Body Language of Customers and Colleagues;* and *Strategic Market Research: A Guide to Conducting Research That Drives Businesses.*

She has told stories all over Chicago in a variety of shows, including Story Lab, Ten by Nine, Is This a Thing, Soul Stories, and The Moth. She is the founder and CEO of Beall Research, a strategic market-research firm. Originally from Massachusetts, she's lived in Chicago for over twenty years and enjoys walking on the lakefront, sampling dark beers, and listening to other storytellers. You can learn more about her on www.AnneBeall.com

Chapter 20 | Love is a Battlefield by Pamela Morgan

One more car among hundreds trapped in a sea of traffic on Lake Shore Drive. Music drifted from somewhere ahead of us. A rhythm I recognized, the sound of the 1980s. A familiar voice, part crooning, part caressing, all rock grit. I glanced in the rear-view mirror to see my son singing along. We'd been driving for two hours, bumper to bumper, for thirty minutes. I was tired, thirsty, hot, and stressed. And I needed a bathroom.

"Love is a battlefield by Pat Benatar!" my son cried, pumping his fist. "This is one of my favorite songs!"

It seemed the whole world had become a battlefield these past few years. For love, not *because* of it.

The earliest battles were him against us. I cringe when I think of it now. My son is transgender, assigned female at birth. But as early as three years old, he began telling us his own opinions on his gender.

Our attack was simple: we knew best, and he didn't. We used our authority and his desire to please us as our weapons. We wielded words like scimitars to slash his defense. How many times did we sit around the dinner table, ganging up on him, bullying him, "Daddy is a boy, Mommy is a girl, you are a…?" Over and over, until he would parrot what we wanted him to say.

How long did it take for his confident answer, "Boy!" to change to a sullen, angry, resentful, "Girl?" Was it six months? A year?

It didn't feel like a victory.

He used his weapons, too. Tears, tantrums, pleas, and finally a heart-wrenching, sobbing request, "Why won't you love me if I'm a boy?"

I told myself it was a retreat. We drew lines.

He could choose his pull-ups and underwear, but not his clothes.

Retreat.

He could choose his clothes, but not his hair style.

Retreat.

He could choose his hair style, but not his pronouns. Not his name.

Retreat.

There came a point in these early battles when I realized I didn't want to be on the other side. I didn't want to be his enemy, his tormentor.

I didn't want to be my child's first bully.

I wanted to love my child unconditionally. To accept him on his own terms, not mine. I did not want to draw lines, make bargains, and constantly feel like enemies on the battlefield.

We battled our families next. Writing letters, we appealed to their common sense and love for our child. We wielded numbers and statistics, rates of suicide, depression, and the horrible, senseless violence against members of the LGBTQ community, but most especially the trans community. We requested that they use male pronouns and a new name out of respect for our child and to support him and us.

We recruited our allies, supporters, people who would defend our child. People who would fight by our side for his rights.

We went in armed and ready to battle his school. We went in with our statistics and our advocates, along with the determination that we must make this place a safe and affirming place for him. This time, they were ready for us. Ready with open arms.

His principal, teacher, and social worker met with us, prepared with videos highlighting the importance of supporting a transitioning student. His teacher had researched strategies to introduce him by his new name and pronouns to his classmates and friends. The principal assured us he would be safe, loved, and welcomed at their school.

That night I wept with relief and fear—for all we had gained and for what still lay ahead.

I knew the real war had finally begun: him against society.

The first wave was the doctors and the therapists—the "professionals," we were told to trust. First there was the pediatrician in 2013, who never followed up with recommendations for therapists, gender clinics, or support groups, despite my many desperate phone calls. There was no one database of resources for children like mine. Sadly, there still isn't for most doctors' offices.

Then, that same year, there was the therapist we found on Psychology Today who promised he was experienced with young children and LGBTQ issues. He grilled my child during the history intake, finally demanding to know what was wrong with girls and why my child didn't want to be one. We marched out of the office on that note, and although he apologized later for his lack of knowledge about trans issues, the damage had been done.

Countless receptionists at so many doctors' offices would call out my son's birth name across a crowded waiting room, despite multiple requests to use the new name. Those attacks did the most damage, emotionally and psychologically. He was outed publicly against his will.

We found allies too.

There was the nurse at the front desk of an urgent care clinic in Joliet, who corrected and scolded her co-worker for misgendering my son. The gastroenterologist told my son he was one special boy, not realizing he was the first medical doctor to affirm his gender identity. And the employee at the hospital who looked up with a steely gaze, when I said that his legal name and gender were not correct and informed her which name and gender we would be using. She deleted his legal name and gender from the system, corrected them, and printed out a wristband for me, my son, and my son's stuffed monkey. "I wouldn't want any mistakes," she said with a curt nod and then smiled.

The second wave of support and backlash came over the internet.

I can attest firsthand that visibility makes a difference. As I met other families like ours, I felt confident in sharing our story publicly. Parents, mothers mostly, reached out to share their stories, to express their fears, to ask for help, or support, or simply wanting a shoulder to cry on. But so did the trolls, with their anonymous vitriol, their judgement and censure. Sometimes they threatened us. I've learned over time to ignore these attacks, but these threats from people who will never know me or my child still frighten and haunt me.

The third and last wave, the constant, unbearable wave, came in the form of government and law. Laws at the time prevented my son from changing his gender marker on his birth certificate unless he hacked off parts of his body permanently. In many states, they still do. Laws also excluded him from bathrooms and locker rooms. Laws insinuated my child, and all trans people, were perverts, sexual predators, and child molesters. Laws such as these encouraged discrimination, segregation, hatred, and violence toward trans people everywhere.

These laws were exhausting to battle but worth the time and effort.

I slammed on the brakes in time to avoid a near collision with the car in front of me. We were a handful of miles from our destination, but the GPS showed another twenty-five minutes. I wasn't sure my bladder could hold out. I cursed silently and glanced at my son in the rearview mirror. He lounged back in his seat with his eyes closed.

Our battle had shifted recently. A new conflict had arisen. My son had reached puberty. Him against himself. We had options, but time was against us. Soon, changes would occur to my son's body that he absolutely did not want. These changes could not be undone. These changes could be paused through medical interventions that were fully reversible and safe. Blockers could give us precious time, years even, for my son to mature before making permanent decisions about his body.

Because his body betrayed him.

Like the insurance company betrayed him, rejecting coverage of these blockers. Rejecting the Lupron shots or Histrelin implant that might very well save my son's life by sparing him the emotional trauma of going through the wrong puberty. Insurance companies rejected my son's gender identity as valid and real, claiming that they weren't medically necessary for treatment of gender dysphoria. This is a battle we fight every year, proving that my son needs and deserves these lifesaving measures to live as himself.

Like our bank accounts betrayed him. We couldn't afford the blockers. They ranged in price from $6,000 to $12,000 a year. Yet we couldn't afford not to get them for him.

It was a three-prong attack, a brilliant maneuver, a concerted effort to eliminate us once and for all. I had spent the better part of the two-hour drive worrying over how we could possibly survive this recent battle unscathed and intact.

Pat Benatar was right. We are strong. We have to be. We have so much farther to go.

I don't know how we win. I don't know if we can win, if we can succeed against the obstacles we have yet to face in this war.

But I know that we must.

I glance once again at the child in the rearview mirror. No, not a child. Young man, who will one day grow up to change the world. I know for his sake, for the sake of all the young people like him, we must be strong and keep fighting.

Wasn't that the point of the song? Love is a battlefield, win or lose, because love is always worth fighting for.

And so is my son's future.

Twenty-three minutes, four miles, and a lifetime to go, but we will never stop fighting.

***

Pamela Morgan is an award-winning playwright and author, who was raised on the South Side of Chicago. Her plays have been produced across the United States and the UK. Pamela's essays have been featured in several anthologies, including *Chicago Storytellers From Stage to Page* (2020), *Here in the Middle*: *Stories of Love, Loss, and Connection from the Ones Sandwiched in Between* (2016), and *So Glad They Told Me: Women Get Real About Motherhood* (2016). In 2024, Amicus Publishing will release her children's picture book, *Simply Skye*, a story about a child exploring gender through their doll. Pamela was first introduced to storytelling in 2015, when her essay, *Best Laid Plans*, was accepted for the Listen to Your Mother live performance in Chicago. She is the proud mother of two amazing children, a member of Dramatist's Guild and Honor Roll. Pamela currently attends the MFA for Creative Writing program at Augsburg University and expects to graduate in 2023. Her website is Pamelamorganwrites.com

Chapter 21 | Body of Phil. *Amen* by Sheri Reda

I always knew that some parts of being Catholic were stupid. Being sentenced to Hell for missing Sunday Mass was stupid. Purgatory wasn't stupid, but reading prayers on holy cards to cut your sentence in Purgatory was stupid. Having to wear a babushka or beanie or doily or even a piece of Kleenex to cover your head was really stupid. But I didn't care. I was willingly entranced and wholly owned by the Roman Catholic Church.

I loved almost everything about being Catholic: the outfits, the colors, the ritual repetition, the rounding of the seasons through the perpetual calendar. I loved how Mass created a sort of sacred space and time. I loved the passion. The weeping. The despair and the joy. I loved the whole show—and hoped to star in it some day, to be one of those saints who might be petitioned aloud in the middle of Sunday Mass.

So when my two best friends, Cory, Jeanmarie, and I developed an abiding crush on the same boy—the same *beee-yooo-tiful* Philip Battaglia—I talked them out of competition in favor of corporate worship. We could be like Joseph of Arimathea and give him a grave!

Phillip Battaglia wasn't dead. He wasn't even sick. But I'd seen headstones for people who were still alive. And if Phillip had a grave, he could have an altar. And if he had an altar, we could go there and pray for him. We could say the rosary, and flick holy water all around, and bring him flowers every day, like in the Rolling Stones song, *Dead Flowers*, the one that went, "I won't forget to put roses on your grave."

And we could pray every day until we prayed his Purgatory away. We'd be perfect Good Samaritans—caring not for his flesh but for his soul. And the most beautiful boy on earth would never even know (until after death) who got him into heaven.

Both Cory and Jeanmarie were in. We began at once.

First, we needed to create a code name. Cory suggested the code word *baseball* because she was rightfully crazy about the 1969 Cubs. But I squashed that.

"It's almost summer, Cory! People will say 'baseball' all the time. We'll go crazy."

Jeanmarie agreed. "Besides, almost anyone could figure out that *Battaglia* begins with *bat*." She suggested *Addison*. "His name's Philip, right? And there's a Saint Phillip in Addison. And Addison is a boy's name! So no one will ever guess."

Cory brightened. "And Wrigley field is *on* Addison Street in Chicago!" she added.

"Yeah," I said. But then I pictured Addison Street in Chicago. It was such a slum, with its beer-bellied factory workers and broken down old two flats.

"But he doesn't deserve Addison Street!" I cried. "We can't burden him with that!"

We tabled the code name until the next day, during science class. We were dutifully pretending to learn the periodic table when the teacher remarked that the symbol for lead was Pb—As in Phillip Battaglia! We didn't know the Pb symbol for lead came from the Latin word meaning "plumb bun," but if we had, we would have been overjoyed. Phillip Battaglia would henceforth be known as Lead. I wrapped up a note, so it resembled a missile, put Cory's and Jeanmarie's names on it, and sent it on through the room.

Once we had a code name for the project, we began our prep work. We went out to the land that had been cleared by Annoreno, a local developer, and chose a well-drained site near the high-tension wires. Then we convened there every day to dig a hole that would be three feet wide by six feet long by six feet deep. We shoveled, and we made wheelbarrows, and we developed ramps, and we got distracted and spent one glorious afternoon cramming ourselves into cardboard boxes and rolling down the ramp.

I lost a tooth rolling down the hill, which was obviously my penance for turning away from the holy task at hand. But Jeanmarie got an even better wound. She had an accident with a nail, which made her look completely crucified in one hand. We revered her stigmata.

And then we knew we were on the right track. We shored up the sides of the grave with the most claylike dirt we could find. We dragged a four by eight sheet of plywood to the site to cover the hole. And then we pounded the cross into the ground just in front of the plywood.

Next, we built an altar with a built-in bookstand and a vase and a place to stash our babushkas, because even though we didn't believe in it, we had to do the cover-your-head thing, or it wouldn't be legitimate. And we were utterly dedicated to this monument of our adoration. It was definitely the summer of love—not only in San Francisco, California— but in Wood Dale, Illinois, too.

My mom occasionally stopped me on my way out to "play." "Why are you carrying a missalette, for God's sake?"

"Yeah!" I agreed, skipping out the door. I was ecstatic. Like Saint Theresa. Possessed with the spirit—of Phil.

Until we got busted. It turned out Mrs. Christian's kitchen window was right across the high-tension wires from our devotional site. Every time we went out to the altar, Mrs. Christian watched us from her kitchen window. We had seen her there—but who cares about a mom at the window doing dishes? Peering into the fields? Maybe she was reminiscing about the days when she, too, roamed free? We paid absolutely no attention to her, except to ponder the inherent meaning in the fact that her name—the name of our witness—was Mrs. Christian.

We never dreamed she would object to our Procession of Lead— starting on the biker's hill and leading down the winding path, underneath the high-tension wires, through the open fields, past the wooded lot, and all the way to the Jewel parking lot. Why should she care about our three wooden crosses made of discarded two by twos nailed together and roped with a sled rope to give them an authentic look? We knew she couldn't see all the way to the memorial class picture, newly adorned each day with fresh dandelions and Queen Anne's Lace. It was, however, possible that she heard the achingly sweet sound of our adapted hymn—*Phil Bataglia-ah, Phil Bataglia-ah, Phil-il-li-ip Ba-ah taglia, In Excelcis Dei-ei-oh.*

Our daily offering was tasteful. It included field-borne beauties like two-tone acorns and abandoned golf balls. Our communion service was devout—*Body of Phil. Amen.* And our prayers were mostly silent.

But she told on us. Mrs. Christian betrayed our private devotions by talking about them in public, in such a way that everybody laughed.

"She's jealous," I told the girls. That's what my mom usually said if someone was mean or rude or a tattletale: They're just jealous.

And if you thought of it, her standing there alone, the wife of a rock-and-roll musician home alone with her six kids, just doing the dishes, while we enjoyed the transcendent, nay, glorious results of our charity—if you thought about it—you could see why Mrs. Christian became our Pontius Pilate.

Word got back to the developer, and he put up a fence, and the fence gained a sign: Property of Annoreno Builders. Keep Out.

Like the early Christians we honored from afar, we were banned from our graveyard devotions. Forced underground—to my cousin's rec room—with the TV blaring Cubs games on WGN. We only got Phillip maybe halfway out of Purgatory.

I wonder if God will let him know why his sentence is so light.

***

Sheri Reda is a writer, presenter, and performer as well as the founder of Flow and Moment, LLC, which offers narrative medicine and writing workshops. She serves on the executive committee of the International Narrative Medicine Institute and on the board of the CG Jung Institute in Evanston. Sheri also co-facilitates the Illinois chapter of the Celebrant Foundation and Institute. Her published works include stories and poems in The Examined Life Journal and The Healer's Burden, by the University of Iowa, and Chicago Storytellers From Stage to Page by Chicago Story Press. Her chapbook entitled, Stubborn was published by Moria Press.

Chapter 22 | A New Journey by Carmenita Peoples

Woohoo! On Saturday, January 11, 2020, Mom made eighty years around the sun! What a blessing. On short notice, we pulled off a small party. Family and friends all piled into her room for the birthday song and well wishes. Her college roommate made the trip from New Orleans. Mom was shocked and delighted when Mama Ella hopped right in the bed to hold her hand, greet family and friends, and tell stories. The *Birthday Queen* was thoroughly adored and grateful for the love and camaraderie. Mama Ella came back the next day for another visit before heading back to New Orleans. As I walked her down the hallway to get her coat, Mama Ella said she'd come back in two weeks. We stared at one another in silence, and I shook my head. Then Mama Ella broke down.

Father Tom came to deliver the last rites on Monday. He took her confession in private, and soon after, he invited us in to listen to a couple of Bible passages. When he finished, Mom said, "Thanks, and see you soon."

Father Tom caught what she said and quickly retorted, "Oh no, not too soon."

We all laughed. The time was drawing nearer. Mom getting last rites, now it was just a waiting game.

Later that night, as we took care of her, a lingering heaviness caught my attention. I stopped, turned around, and looked up. An amalgamation of black silhouettes blanketed the ceiling. The ancestors were gearing up for the *real* party and they were in full force. I saw my grandparents, my uncles and aunts, and mom's best friends at this reception. Overwhelmed, I took a deep breath. This was happening, and in a flash, it was time for me to pass the baton. No more picking up meds from CVS, making extra green drinks and meals, and *Jeopardy* afternoons, no more doctors' appointments, no more singing and dancing, no more—Mama?

I reflected on the fact that Mom lived an exceptionally invigorating life. She was a business owner a few times over and took life by the horns. She lived by her own rules and created a place for herself when others said there was none. Mom was co-owner of three McDonald's restaurants with my dad and survived the banking crash of the early nineties. I loved seeing her in action; people didn't know what hit them, but it was in the best way! She could talk herself into or out of any situation, a sharp cookie with powerful leadership and resolve. So, this was just another thing for her to conquer, or so I thought.

On Tuesday, I contacted a dear friend, our shared spiritual counselor, to help pray Mom into paradise. She came in the afternoon and spent private time with Mom, and I left to go Uber. After eighteen months of fighting the deadly disease, I couldn't sit around until her last breath. I knew in my heart when I gave her that kiss goodbye, it would be the last.

My rides had me all over the city, and I ended up in the northwest suburbs. Ride after ride I was quiet, offering minimal conversation, which is not like me. I am usually quite engaging with my riders. I was focusing on my breath. I didn't receive any phone calls, so I stayed in the streets. I figured no news was better.

Around 8:00 pm that night, I found myself at the Naf Naf Grill in Schaumburg, trying to grab some dinner. My sister called; she was frantic. She was having difficulty waking Mom, who seemed cold. She begged me to come home right away. My stomach sank. This was the final curtain call. As I drove down I-294, my mind raced a million miles a second. I was so anxious, and I tried to breathe.

My mind played vignettes of Mom, me, and my family. It was like *This Is Your Life* in pixilation. This was the day new memories with Mom would cease to be made. And as I came up on I-94 approaching Hubbard's cave, I got a ping. I forgot to turn off the damn Uber app! In an instant, I accepted the ride and jumped off at Randolph. I needed someone to fill my car with their energy and give me something else to focus on before I went home.

My rider was visiting Chicago, and he was so excited to meet up with friends at Buddy Guy's Legends on Wabash. He was asking about different music, places to hang out, and then he asked how my evening was going.

I lied and forced a smile, replying, "Great. You're my last ride."

The last ride of an Uber shift is always a time for celebration, but not tonight. I didn't want to let him out of the car. His joyful spirit put me at ease, if only for the eight minutes he rode with me. He reminded me that *everything* in life is temporary, and what I was about to experience was also, temporary. After he got out of the car, I let out an enormous sigh and drove south toward Balbo and Lake Shore Drive.

An uncommonly huge, bright moon shone across the lake offering the *Golden Path* to the heavens. And I received it as such. I thought about this VIP treatment the ancestors set up for Mom's reception. And rightfully so because everything she did was top of the line. Immediately I raved, "Thank you, Mama, thank you for everything. You're my very best Mom."

It was one of our running jokes, and she'd always reply, Girl, I'm your only Mama!"

The Point blocked the moon, but as I passed the Museum of Science and Industry, it was prevalent again. As I came over the small hill, I felt my body, where my womb is, expel a tremendous rush of energy. It erupted out of me. It overtook my body. I struggled but couldn't find my breath. I howled and laughed and shook my head. It was absolute loneliness. Mama was making her big journey and came to tell me goodbye.

The job that I held for so long, caring for mom, was done. Where is all the religiosity I've studied to get me through this? I summoned all the prophets at once. In the next instant, I saw my mom in the arms of her mother. I found my breath. Holding the image that she was returning to pure love kept me from losing total control.

In the last mile and a half to my home, there was a resounding peace that came over me. And I knew my mom was kicking it with all those ancestors who had been preparing for her the night before. I was sure that she was getting the *Welcome to Paradise* Platinum Package.

I parked in the garage, took a few deep breaths, and started up the stairs to hear the news.

My sister raced down the stairs, grabbed me, and tearfully said, "She's gone, she's gone."

I simply replied, "Thank you, God."

I was overwhelmingly grateful. She wasn't in any more pain.

Thank you, thank you... Thank you!

***

Carmenita Peoples is an artistic performer, writer, and certified Montessori educator. She currently serves as part-time staff and educational contractor at the University of Chicago Lab Schools. Her company, Innovative Art and Education, LLC, works with students, parents, and teachers to offer specialized programming, education, and support through performance art. As a graduate of The Second City Training Center musical conservatory, improv and writing programs, Carmenita uses her artistry to bridge inter-cultural and generational gaps. She is also a writer, producer, and director of children's plays. Carmenita has performed at The Moth, Write Club, Story Jam, Story Serenade, and Soul Stories. A dreamer, a seeker, a mother, and a friend, Carmenita "edutains" audiences throughout the city of Chicago and its surrounding suburbs. She is one of the featured storytellers in *Chicago Storytellers From Stage to Page*. Her mantra is, "Let's connect through our stories."

Chapter 23 | Tainted Love by JC Quigley

We met online. We texted for over a month and our banter had been fun, but in that slightly sexy sort of way. I sensed he might be another *bad boy*, and I had a long history of being attracted to bad boys. Bad boys have a certain seductive edge and a precise charm. They are confident, aggressive, and typically completely narcissistic. They are used to getting their way. Of course, I was attracted to the game and their confidence was my aphrodisiac. I wanted to understand why I was drawn to this tragic type of man, like bees are drawn to honey, but where the honey was always an illusion and my soul always got stung. Maybe, just maybe, he wasn't a bad boy. So I agreed to meet him.

It was October 2019 when I moved back to Chicago. I spent the last twenty years on the East Coast, two divorces in my rear-view mirror, mother of two grown kids. I was living *alone* for the first time in a long time. I could now focus on reigniting my career in corporate America, having taken a few years off to support my daughter while she battled her own demons to finish high school. I loved melting into the bustle of my morning commute on the L walking to my big office on West Madison full of my new legion of friendly colleagues. I had been sequestered away in my suburban mom role for far too long, and I wanted my old self back— the unfettered, slightly wild twenty something who began her career in Chicago. I wanted to pick up the pieces of myself I had lost, discover how I fit into this new world, and find out how I had changed.

Two months later, now mid-December 2019, I met the man who had intrigued me the most. He kept me interested with his intermittent texting and subtle sexual innuendo. He created this heightened sense of uncertainty that led to my excitement and anxiety, a lethal combination.

I walked into the crowded, loud downtown bar where we agreed to meet. I looked around and didn't see anyone who resembled the picture he sent me earlier, so I went to the end of the bar. I ordered a drink. Ten minutes passed. I told myself I would leave if he didn't show within ten minutes or before I finished my wine, whichever occurred first. I wondered if this was part of his game—to keep me waiting. I'm sure it was.

He arrived before my self-imposed departure time, and I recognized him immediately when he walked behind me and casually took a seat at the bar. He had a nicely defined jaw and a slightly stubbled beard, a broad, slightly Neanderthalic forehead and nose, dark narrow eyes and thin lips that turned into a soft smile. I smiled slightly and shook my head at him. Of course, I was attracted to him.

He ordered a drink, and we immediately started talking. He told me he was divorced, over fifty, and had two kids. It's not what was on his profile. When I asked what led to his divorce, he coolly told me he and his ex-wife stopped having sex. He took a sip of his drink and then offered it to me. I drank it.

We didn't stay long. He said he had to leave. It was his night with his kids. As we left the bar, he offered to give me a ride home. He had an expensive car with leather seats and a door that closed softly. The ride home was quick, and he stopped in front of my building. I looked at him, but he didn't move to kiss me. As I got out of his car, I said goodbye and thanked him for the ride. I was both slightly drunk and very enamored.

He texted me the next day and said I was beautiful and that he wanted to see me again. I responded that he could take me out again sometime soon. But he didn't. He continued to text me at random times to keep the connection going, but never asked me to go out again.

A few days before Christmas, he hinted he wanted to come over. I knew exactly what he wanted but didn't want to acknowledge he was *not available*. His seduction tactics worked. If I said yes to him and let him come over, sex would happen. His skill in the art of seduction and my craving to be seen, validated, and desired pushed me beyond the precipice of good judgment or reason. It didn't even matter anymore. I wanted this man.

On the evening of New Year's Day, I agreed to let him come over. I met him outside of my apartment, my dog in tow, and kissed him. We walked up the stairs to my apartment and went immediately into my bedroom. We did not waste any time or words. Then he left. And then I let it happen a few more times over the next two months. The intensity was built on his unpredictable texting and visits. And then I became miserable because I was stuck in the thick of the illusionary honey, and my soul was getting stung. So much for my big experiment to learn more about this instinctual draw to bad boys; it had gone way off the rails.

My feelings of guilt and shame overwhelmed me. I did not want to be on this ride that was taking me to the bottom of a deep, dark well of despair. I decided to end it in person. On his next visit, I confronted him. He denied he was married. But I knew, and he knew, that I knew.

He sent me a text after he left, "See ya round, kid. BTW, you are amazing."

The world fell apart when the pandemic hit full stride in March 2020. I tried to forget him. I began dating another man but became restless after a few months. I dipped my toe into the wild west of the dating apps—Tinder. When I pressed the button to go live, he found me quickly. We started again shortly thereafter. I ended my other relationship.

With the pandemic and the Chicago riots as a backdrop, we continued to see each other that spring and summer of 2020 and into the next year. His random texts became more predictable in their randomness, our time together became more predictable, condensed, and intense. I struggled with the intensity of my feelings. I broke up with him on two more occasions when I felt I was getting too emotionally attached. I realized how easily men could detach from their emotions in sexual relationships. I tried to detach, but repeatedly failed.

It was now the beginning of July 2021. I decided to move back to the East Coast. Nothing was holding me in this city of big shoulders. I accepted a new position where I worked from home. I was drawn back to the ocean and the vast sandy beaches of the South Shore of Massachusetts, my old friends, and the familiar seaside communities where my kids grew up. When things get hard, or my relationships get difficult or fall apart, I am inclined to move. My heart was breaking.

I alternated between sadness and relief, sandwiched between apprehension, anxiety, and lack of clarity. I knew if I stayed, nothing would change. He was the one who made me feel the way I wanted to feel when I moved to Chicago—unfettered, wild, sexy, wanted. I loved that he wanted me so intensely—even though it was just physical. I didn't really know him. The entire narrative of our relationship had taken place within the four walls of my bedroom. I could not continue.

When I told him I was leaving, he froze as he lay in my bed next to me. I could see his eyes well up. Then he said, "Wow." And then he was quiet while he let it sink in. He quickly regained his composure, got up, got dressed, and told me he wanted to see me at least one more time before I left. And then he was gone. Just like always.

I wanted to tell him, "I love you. I always have. You felt familiar to me from the very beginning. I knew I would like you before I met you. You knew the seduction game better than anyone. I wanted to be special, an impossibility given the circumstances and your inability or refusal to allow yourself to have any feelings. I will never get what I always wanted from you. That is why our relationship, or whatever you want to call it, worked so well. It was based on constant need and longing. Needs like ours are tragic; we chase the illusion because we know the reality can never live up to the dream. And dreams are enormously powerful."

My days were blurring as I got ready to leave. I prepared myself for our last encounter. I knew he would act like nothing was happening. I resolved not to give myself away to him. I would not confess my love, sadness, or real feelings. None of these things belonged in this space with him. When he came over, it was just like every other time we were together. Afterward, he walked to the door of my bedroom that opened up to my back patio, the one he always used to enter my apartment. We kissed at the door, and I said I didn't like goodbyes, and that I'd see him later, that he would be in my head. He looked at me and said, "likewise." He kissed me and left.

I always knew I was playing a rigged game. But I learned from him. I learned about how I could absolutely hide my vulnerability and pretend not to want anything when I really wanted everything. Even if I had told him I wanted everything, I knew his answer. I knew we had created a fantasy that would not last in the real world. Perhaps that was the ultimate tragedy. I wondered if intense pleasure was dependent solely on the dysfunction that exists between two damaged souls, creating a symphony of hollow notes that disappear as soon as they are heard.

I missed him already. I missed his texts, his passion, his smell, his consistent inconsistency. We were each other's drug. I couldn't say goodbye yet.

Chicago will always remind me of him. He occupied more of my mind than I ever wanted. I walked the streets of the city with my dog and always felt like he was watching me. I cried. I despaired. I fantasized. I tried to leave. But this time he couldn't bring me back with a simple irresistible text. He cannot bring me back.

At the end of July, I left Chicago with my dog and packed car. I cried throughout the state of Indiana. I knew it would be painful, as it always was when I tried to leave. I knew it would pass. I let it go. I let the pain in. Our physical connection was intense. I loved it and hated it. It gave me this fleeting hit of massive pleasure, then the crash. Highly intoxicating, destructive, massively addictive, synthetic love. I wondered when I would hear from him again. I knew I was headed in a better direction.

I drove for eighteen hours with just a few short breaks and headed immediately to my friend's house. It was the soft landing I needed. I took a shower and spent the rest of the day with them. I was finally home. I had escaped.

***

JC Quigley is the pen name for the author of this story, who wishes to protect her privacy. She now resides in a small coastal town in Massachusetts with her dog. She is so happy to be closer to her grown children, her friends, and the ocean and beaches that fill her soul with joy, peace, and wonder. She started journaling about her dating experiences when she moved to Chicago and was encouraged to take a writing class by her dear friend George. This led her to Jill Howe and her amazing classes held remotely during the pandemic shutdown at the Newberry Library. She continues journaling about her life experiences, including musings about dating beyond middle age, desire, feminism, and exploring and challenging herself to become more fearless in every way.

Chapter 24 | Travels with Charlie by Julie Danis

My dad took a banana boat to Cuba. He was a twenty-four-year-old bachelor on an adventure before he joined the family construction company. He told me about this trip one Sunday afternoon when an impeccably dressed young man in a blue blazer with gold buttons visited our house. I recall the man spoke English with an accent, and his visit had something to do with Cuba, because that's when Dad started talking banana boats.

"They shipped bananas north from South America to the United States, and people instead of bananas went south," Dad said.

As an eight-year-old, I couldn't imagine Dad on a banana boat. My father came home for dinner every night after work, made up stories with characters resembling his own children, and attended Mass every Sunday—even on vacations.

"Travel when you can," Dad said.

That was in 1963, and I knew two things about Cuba: it was communist, and no one could travel there. But my dad managed to go there on a banana boat.

Dad died when I was forty. When I cleaned out his chest of drawers, I found his pictures from Cuba, among other keepsakes, like his Omega watch and St. Christopher Medal. In one photo, he overlooked an old-world plaza from a baroque wrought-iron balcony with a whimsical curlicue design. A church, with a round stained-glass window in its steeple above the bell tower, stood in the background. Cars with bloated hoods, trunks, and fenders—straight out of an Al Capone movie—lined the plaza.

On the back of the picture, Dad wrote, "Me again overlooking the city of Havana, Cuba from the balcony of a den of iniquity where we had been having a drink or two. 1939."

Dad always said, "Write on the back of your pictures or else you'll never remember where you were or who you were with."

Dad had been dead for sixteen years in 2012 when my husband Paul and I boarded a plane to Cuba with a group from the Goodman Theatre. We were part of a people-to-people tour, promoting cultural and educational exchange. Our itinerary included seeing a play at Teatro Buendia, visiting a folk-dance school, and touring Hemingway's estate.

I didn't know what to expect. Outdated images and impressions of life under Castro's reign filled my head. Oppression. Military police. Government stores and shortages. I wondered if I would see the same things Dad saw and feel the same way he felt. I packed the photo and prayed I might at least find the building with the balcony, where he stood seventy-three years ago.

"You know we can't veer off our Department of State approved itinerary," Paul reminded me.

He was right. We had to sign an official document that said we would not stray from our plans. But I thought Dad would want me to try.

Family lore says that I wouldn't have anything to do with my father until I turned three. Then I wouldn't leave him alone. As a little girl, I danced on his wingtip shoes. As a teen, I drove him to his office, where I worked as a receptionist. As an adult, I slept in his hospital room and fed him ice chips before he died. Dad had been gone sixteen years, but I wasn't done being his daughter, keeping him alive through his stories, or doing things that brought a bit of his past into my present.

By the time our plane landed, everyone in our group knew my father had been to Havana. Maria, a fellow traveler and Cuban-American who left Cuba as a ten-year-old in 1960, recognized the church in the picture as la Catedral de San Cristobal, but she didn't know the building.

When I showed the picture to Osvaldo, our Cuban tour guide, his eyes widened in disbelief. When I read the "den of iniquity" inscription on the back, he blushed from the neck of his blue blazer to his jet-black hairline.

"This is Plaza de la Catedral," Osvaldo said. "We will be walking through there after lunch."

"Today, we're going to see it? Today? Do you know the building in the picture?" I asked.

"Si. I don't remember a balcony, but there is a museum across from the church. It was formerly a governor's mansion."

"Can we visit it?" I asked excitedly.

"I believe it is closed. But we'll see."

I felt sorry for Osvaldo. It was the first hour of the first day of the tour, and someone had already asked him for a favor. Me. But this was the square where my dad had taken his picture. If not now, when? I felt like a kid at Christmas waiting to see if Santa brought the one present I wanted most. I was ready to burst.

But before we went to the square, our group walked along the Malecon, the cracked concrete and stone waterfront promenade that runs along the Havana Harbor. We tromped up the steps of the Castillo de la Real Fuerza to its ramparts. In the Plaza de Armas, we photographed Cuban school children wearing the red kerchiefs and shorts or suspender skirts they have worn since the 1960s. We browsed bookstalls that sold pamphlets covered with stern images of Lenin, Che, and Castro.

We stopped for a lunch of pollo cubano y arroz con frijoles in a restaurant that catered to tourists. Serenading musicians gave ladies roses, and dancers wearing swirls of color wove through the tables, enticing camera-laden patrons to the dance floor. I watched all this activity thinking, *When can we go to the plaza?*

After lunch, we strolled along cobblestone streets for what seemed like miles. Sights and sounds stopped us at every turn. The beats of an Afro-Cuban jazz trio played in front of a storefront with peeling yellow paint and stucco. A rainbow of taxis—restored American classic cars like

Ford Fairlanes, Buick Roadmasters, and Chevrolet Deluxes—lined up in front of a down-on-its-luck hotel. A parade of dancers on stilts engulfed us in their joyful progression down the street. Over the cacophony, I heard Osvaldo say, "Julie, look ahead."

There, in front of me, was a plaza and a church. I pulled the picture from my backpack, held it up, and compared the image with reality. Café tables with Cinzano umbrellas filled the plaza instead of cars. A twelve-foot-high red and white heart sat to one side of the church in celebration of upcoming Valentine's Day. Across from the church stood a two-story building, with two windows on each side of a central entranceway. A baroque wrought-iron balcony with a whimsical curlicue design decorated each opening.

"Paul, look!" I said, bouncing on my toes and waving the picture in his face. "That's the building with the balcony! It actually exists."

It was the Museo de Arte Colonial, which was under restoration. The facade looked preserved, compared to most of the buildings in Havana, which were crumbling, flaking, or missing complete sections. The balconies and front door were painted a cerulean blue. One glance inside the open entrance gate revealed a courtyard full of rubble, beams, and hard hats.

A young guard, wearing an army-green uniform, white gloves, and a frown, sat on a metal chair at the entrance. Osvaldo explained I wanted to go inside while I showed her the picture.

"Go upstairs, por favor? Mi papi, por favor?" I pleaded. She responded in short spurts but didn't acquiesce.

Maybe she didn't understand how old the photo was, or that the man in the picture was my dad. She didn't seem to appreciate that I had a chance to recreate history. In hindsight, she probably thought I was another pushy American tourist flocking to the once forbidden island.

Dad had a way of getting invited into buildings. Not pushy, but in a confident, friendly way. He would hold out his hand and introduce himself, "Hi, Charlie Danis, Dayton, Ohio." We, his family, would walk through model homes that weren't open or take pictures of a Ponderosa Steakhouse that was under renovation—while on vacation. But I was not Dad.

"She has no authority," Osvaldo said. As the daughter of a builder, I understood that construction sites were hazard zones. I was disappointed, but at least we had found the building.

"You have a little time to take photos outside," Osvaldo said.

While the rest of the group explored the church or had a Cuban coffee under the shade of an umbrella, Paul and I moved to the right side of the entrance. A construction worker—with skin creased by age and sun, wearing paint-splattered overalls—sat in the first-floor window, right below the balcony, smoking a cigarette.

"Mi Papi," I said, showing him the picture and pointing from the picture to me to the balcony. "1939."

"Papi?"

"Si, mi Papi"

"Ah, Papi!"

Paul snapped pictures of me in front of the balcony. Close-up and long shots of the balcony and ones of me from every angle.

"Senora," the construction worker said. He pointed to the balcony, to me, to the entrance, to my camera, and then disappeared.

A few seconds later, I heard a voice. "Senora, Senora." The construction worker was standing at the entrance signaling, "Come now, come fast."

The guard stood up and held her hand out to stop us, but the construction worker said something in Spanish that I have decided meant, "I'm taking her inside. No one will mind, please." He took my hand, and we scurried over rocks and picked our way through the crumbled, faded glory of the inner courtyard.

I was transported back to a day when I was thirteen, touring a downtown job site with Dad. Wearing matching yellow hard hats, he guided me by the hand around sawhorses, concrete forms, and pieces of rebar on the top of what would be the tallest building in Dayton. From the thirtieth floor we scanned the skyline. He pointed out buildings—churches, schools, and warehouses—that the company his dad started had built.

"Julie," he said, "girls can be engineers. You can study engineering and work for the company."

Dad's greatest dream was to have his children, daughters, and sons follow in his footsteps. This was his path to happiness, and he just wanted me to be happy. Even if I didn't become an engineer, and I didn't, I felt his belief in me and all that I could become.

Paul and I were ushered into a room off the second-floor gallery. A smiling, matronly guard offered to hold my purse. In a photo frenzy, Paul captured my balcony moments: pictures of me holding Dad's photo and then just pictures of me. Close-up and far away. In the same pose as Dad, and not the same pose. My face lit with a toothy smile as I realized I was experiencing a part of Dad's past.

I don't know how long I stood on that balcony, emotion flooding my being, trying to emblazon the scene and this moment into my memory. I think I *talked* to Dad, maybe through a prayer. I do know I felt the joy that a daughter of any age feels when she's sharing something special with her dad.

"Julie," Paul whispered, breaking into my thoughts, "it's time."

The cathedral bell tolled, and I said a prayer of thanks to San Cristobal, or St. Christopher, the patron saint of travelers, for his intervention in this journey. It would have been just like Dad to seek his help: "Hi, I'm Charlie Danis and I'd like to share a balcony with my daughter."

***

Julie M. Danis is a writer, storyteller, and former marketing/advertising executive. As a business humorist, she wrote a *Chicago Tribune* column called *It's a Living* and contributed commentary to *Marketplace* radio. She was a writer for the award-winning documentary film, *The Girl Who Wore Freedom,* a love story between French citizens and World War II veterans. Her essays have been published in the *Huffington Post, More*, and *Life Reimagined* (now part of AARP.org). She has told stories at live events in Chicago, such as The Moth, Story Club, Story Lab, and 2nd Story.

During her business career, she probed consumers' minds to understand why they did what they did. She's conducted global studies on the future of food, technology, Gen Y, and humor in advertising. She was an adjunct lecturer at Northwestern University's Medill School and is a graduate of the Second City School of Improvisation. Her favorite title was Director of Mind and Mood.

Chapter 25 | Love, Loyalty, and the Kiss that Sealed Our Fate by Debra Taitel

Imagine glancing across a crowded room and locking eyes with a person who instantly makes your heart explode. The connection is undeniable. In an instant, those big brown eyes pierce the walls of protection you've carefully set up around your heart.

Then imagine that shortly after, the person slowly makes their way across the room, smiles at you, and says, "Hey, Debbie, can I borrow a pencil?" Yes, those were the words that melted my heart at seven years old. They were also the words that started my journey of love.

At the time, I thought, *Oh my God, Mike S borrowed a pencil. He likes me!* Followed by, *We're gonna get married one day!*

When I love, I love fiercely, unapologetically, and with all my being, and although I don't fall in love easily, when I do, I fall hard.

I never stopped thinking about this cute boy with the big brown eyes, late 1960s bowl haircut, and an impish smile. He looked like a cross between the innocent, fun-loving Davy Jones from The Monkees and the cunning Jack Wild, as the Artful Dodger in the 1968 movie version of *Oliver*.

Mike and I were friends throughout grammar school, but he never gave me the ID bracelet engraved with his name that told the world we were going steady, a common practice in the late 1960s and early 1970s. It was, as they say, unrequited love, but I didn't care. I loved him just the same.

In my mind, just like those love stories that only happen in movies and Broadway musicals, our love story would last forever. This was the story we would tell our friends, children, and grandchildren. We would tell them we met in first grade, and our love started with him borrowing a pencil.

When I was in seventh grade, my family moved from Des Plaines to Northbrook, Illinois. I was devastated that we were moving away from the love of my life, but I had to accept it. I went on to a new junior high school, made new friends, and even had a few boy crushes, but I always wondered what would have happened if we never moved. My first love was a fading memory that would only come to the forefront when a cute boy asked to borrow a pencil, which happened from time to time.

Once I entered high school, there were more new friends and new boys. I had crushes on Victor, David, Russ, and John, but as high school romances usually are, they were short-lived. As a hopeful romantic, I knew my next love would show up. I did not know how or when, but somehow, I knew.

And then, when I was seventeen, it happened.

I received a call from my best friend, Joan. She had just dropped out of high school and was enrolled in night school to get her GED. She met this great guy in one of her GED classes, whom she thought would be perfect for me. She said he was cute and funny. He wore a leather jacket and had a muscle car, as was popular in the late 1970s. Best of all, he had a job. Hey, these things matter to a teenage girl!

Joan said they had been hanging out, she told him about me, and he was interested in meeting. We planned a meet-up for the following Friday night at a local forest preserve. Now I got excited. I finally asked, "What is his name?" Joan casually replied, "Mike S."

Wait, what? Could it possibly be the *same* Mike S? No, it could not be. I asked Joan to ask if he grew up in Des Plaines and if he had gone to Nathanson Grammar School.

He did. At seventeen, I was about to go on a date with my first love! It felt surreal, as if I was floating on a cloud. I was excited, nervous, and terrified. I carefully planned, checked, and double-checked what I would wear and how I would do my hair and make-up. I needed this night to be *perfect*.

When Friday came, I could barely breathe. My head was spinning with thoughts of my Prince Charming, also known as Mike S, wearing a black-leather jacket, riding up on his white horse, or in this case his red-muscle car. I dreamed of us riding off into the sunset.

It didn't matter I had not seen him in over ten years or that we were no longer carefree, seven or eight-year-olds. No, this was much better. We were teenagers, ready to take on the world!

I hopped into my Pontiac Firebird and headed to the forest preserve. I spotted my girlfriend amongst all the cars and high school kids. We waited.

Before long, we heard the low rumble of a finely tuned muscle car. My heart beat so hard I thought it would come out of my chest. Mike waved and parked his car farther down, in a spot where it would not get dinged by another vehicle.

Well, this is it, I thought. I took a deep breath and watched him get out of his car. The first thing I noticed was the leather jacket and boots. He looked like a throwback to the 1950s. He had slick, greased-back hair. Not the style of the time. When he finally stood in front of me, I realized it was not the greased-back hair of the 1950s; it was dirty, greasy hair that smelled like a combination of sweat, motor oil, and raging hormones. I did not expect him to look the same as he did years ago. But I expected him to smell better

We hung out with a few friends drinking Boones Farm Strawberry Wine and Mad Dog 20/20 wine, and then we went to his car for a less superficial conversation. It turned out we had very different backgrounds. He was still cute, but I quickly realized our different perspectives and views of life would be challenging at best to bring together. We talked for a while before he put his arm around me and leaned in for a kiss. This kiss was the one I dreamed of since I was seven! A kiss that sealed our fates once and for all.

To say it was a bad kiss was an understatement. He did not just kiss my mouth; he kissed and slobbered on my entire face. I almost laughed at how disgusting that kiss was. Although I have kissed my fair share of boys and men, to this day, I have not experienced another kiss as bad as that.

I calmly composed myself and made some excuse to leave. I never saw or heard from Mike S again. Of course, looking back on it now, I laugh at the sweet thoughts of my seven-year-old self and slightly cringe at the memory of our first and last date. I have a wonderful memory of loving that little, brown-eyed boy who borrowed my pencil, and to be honest, I still love the memory of him. Loving someone at seven or seventy is the best feeling in the world, and even if it is not to be a grand love affair that lasts forever, it is no less significant. You never forget your first love, and if you think about it, love never ends. It simply changes as we gain wisdom from growth and experience.

And I will add that I truly believe the essence of the Tennyson quote, "'Tis better to have loved [and moved on] than never to have loved at all."

***

Debra F. Taitel is not only a writer, she is a reader—a clairvoyant reader. Her readings and meditation classes help guide people to more fully access their gift of clarity and to connect with their highest essence and creative expression.

Debra's published work first appeared in 2009 on her blog *Daily Muse, A Clairvoyant Look at Daily Life.* Her insightful musings offer a different perspective for those looking to change their lives. Her blog has received accolades from authors and spiritual teachers around the world.

Debra fell in love with crafting personal narrative stories when she recognized that storytelling is transformative both for the artist and the audience. Debra has told stories at various Chicago shows including, Pour One Out, DB Comedy, Story Jam, and StoryLab Chicago. She has been a frequent guest on podcasts and radio shows including, *Cosmic Tuesdays* and *The Jill Dahne Show.* She has also appeared as the featured guest on *Ester Goldberg TV* with Ester Goldberg.

In her free time, you will find Debra enjoying the Chicago arts scene, teaching meditation and clairvoyant classes, or snuggling with her gorgeous kitty, Venus.

Website: https://spiritlightinsight.com/
Instagram: https://www.instagram.com/spiritlightinsight/
Facebook Personal: https://www.facebook.com/debbie.taitel/

Chapter 26 | Dad by Jonathan Euseppi

Two people I respect are Deepak Chopra and my father. Deepak Chopra once said that happiness is the continuation of events that are not resisted. One of my dad's favorite quotes was, "Get this goddamn dog away from me!"

Some dads threaten to take the belt out, but my dad threatened to pistol whip... the couch. He would stub his toe and yell, "Goddamn! Goddamn! Goddamn! I'm going to pistol whip this motherfucker!" And he didn't even own a gun. So we would look at Mom and she would say, "He's fine. He's just in pistol-whip mode."

He was one of those dads that would get so angry that he couldn't talk. He would grab his waistband, growl like a grizzly in dress slacks, and just walk out of the house.

"Where is he going?" we would ask Mom.

"He's driving."

"Where to?"

"Just... driving."

Where he would go was to Taco Bell. We grew up in El Paso, Texas with some of the best Mexican food in the world. But that wasn't where my dad was going. He would fly right past those places and go straight to Taco Bell. This was the 1990s Taco Bell. In those days, the bell looked like a setting sun because they were not trying to hide that this place was sad. You would walk in and say, "I am trying not to feel!" And they would say, "Do you want a paper briefcase of tacos or burritos?"

"Give me both! Goddamn it!" my dad would say.

My dad's anger was the biggest issue we had growing up. I never knew why he was angry, and as a result, I harbored a lot of anger toward him. I always wanted to do normal father-son things with him, but we could never get there because we would get sabotaged by his anger. I remember one time we were supposed to build a basketball goal together, and he ended up calling Sports Authority and threatened to pistol whip the entire staff.

Another time, he taught me how to mow the lawn.

"Alright, John. Stand up straight. I've got to teach you some shit. Why are your hands in your pockets? You playing pocket pool?"

I stared at him, afraid to speak.

"It means you are touching your dick. Alright, never mind. To start it, you have to turn the lever to green. You watchin? You pull this back. Here we go."

Dad pulled the cord three times, but the engine sputtered to a stop.

"The goddamn thing is flooded. When the thing gets flooded, you have to push this little knob right here. Get some gas going through the engine. Alright. Here we go."

Dad stepped backwards right into a pile of dog shit.

"Oh, goddamn it, John, I stepped in shit! There must be forty pieces of shit in the goddamn yard. I can't teach you to mow the lawn when there's shit everywhere. You clean up the shit, and I'll start the motherfucker!"

Dad pulled the cord over and over again. Watching him was like watching a chemical reaction that once started, could not be stopped.

"Goddamn, goddamn! Goddamn! You lousy motherfucker!"

He picked up the lawn mower and spun it around like an Olympian in the hammer throw competition, but this spin was erratic and filled with unfocused rage. After two spins, he got enough momentum to launch the lawn mower across the yard.

"John!... John?"

I was frozen, terrified of what would come next, but I gathered the courage to look at him.

"That's how you mow the lawn."

The day my dad died, he was riding his motorcycle back from Las Cruces, New Mexico to our home in El Paso. He often did this ride on the weekends with some friends. They would cruise, have lunch, and then ride back home. He loved this ride because he would take a two-lane highway that cut through beautiful farmland, which reminded him of his childhood.

He grew up on a farm in Arkansas on an isolated piece of land. He had a Catholic-Italian family. His own father was not religious. In fact, the family jokingly called my grandfather, *The Good Book* because he always used the lord's name in vain. My grandmother was a sweet, plump Italian mother who just wanted to feed everyone. My father had two brothers and three sisters. His brothers took over the farm, but my father left to pursue his dreams.

He was on this two-lane highway that reminded him of his childhood when he began to pass a car. Somehow, his motorcycle went off the road. I have seen the tracks. He almost got back on the road, but something happened, and he went over the handlebars. His 800-pound motorcycle came down upon him, crushed his face, his ribs, all his organs, and snapped his neck. And just like that, he was dead.

After he died, I learned so much about him. I found out that he finally went to therapy. When my mom was separating from him, she said, "Ned, I can't take this anymore. I am going to therapy." And he became more frightened than he had ever been in his entire life. He never thought in a million years that she would leave him.

"You're going to therapy? Well, I'm going to fucking therapy!" he yelled.

So he went to therapy out of spite. But he went. At the funeral, the therapist told my mother that my dad would come into his office and just cry. This really shocked me. He was so scary, that I never realized he was hurting. I found out that his father, the Good Book, had been in World War II, had PTSD, and was an alcoholic. One time, he came into the living room with a rifle and my dad had to fight him to protect the family. Things like this happened so often that my dad had undiagnosed PTSD. I found out that when my mom and dad were separated, the people in the apartment complex where he was living threw him a party where he announced he was going to get his family back. I found out these things and it totally changed how I viewed him.

What haunts me about his death was that it happened so suddenly. The day he died, he dropped me off at the mall. Before I got out of the car, he turned to me and said, "John, I love you."

I said nothing.

I was so angry at him before he died that I thought if I ignored him long enough and shamed him hard enough, he would change. I realized after he died that was a complete waste of our time together. And I so wish that I could say something that would make him feel lovely, and seen, and at peace.

I wish I could talk to him in one of our moments where we tried to connect but were blocked by his rage. Just when he was about to throw the lawn mower across the yard, I wish I had said, "Dad, this isn't going well, but I want you to know that I love you even though you fight all of our appliances all the time. I think you are very smart, and you have a big heart, and you are very funny. And when you sit down and play cards, you make everyone happy. I don't know why you are doing these things, but I don't hate you. I love you."

***

Jonathan Euseppi is a storyteller, stand-up comedian, and improviser. He is best known for his storytelling style, which tackles intense subjects while holding them in a loving and humorous way. His one-person show, *Grief is Horny* won the Staff Pick for Best in Fringe at the 2019 San Francisco Fringe Festival. He has been seen performing stories at City Winery and the Gibbs Morrison Cultural Center. He recently completed a successful run on his one-person show, *Cancer is Gorgeous* at the Crowd Theater in Chicago. When not performing, Jonathan enjoys spending time with his wife Katie and their two cats, Don and Chubbs.

Chapter 27 | Coming of Age in an Urban Bubble by Dan Terkell

In the Spring of 1963, I was a high-school senior with a part-time job at a family-operated supermarket, Broadway Finer Foods, on Chicago's North Side. The neighborhood known as Lake View, in my youth, was largely made up of working-class folks except for a ribbon of prosperity along Lake Shore Drive. Over the decades, the entire area has become gentrified.

Broadway Finer Foods always had fifteen or twenty part-time workers like me, with an equal number of girls and boys. The girls worked the registers at the check-out counters. The guys kept the shelves stocked and helped the ladies bag groceries whenever needed.

A new girl magically appeared behind a register one Saturday morning toward the end of March. In an instant, I was smitten! She was petite, with thick raven hair long enough to get lost in. Her glasses had black plastic frames, very much like mine. Facial outbreaks occasionally plagued her, but I fought that same fight, too. Above all, we were both nerds. Her name was Eleni.

Neither of us was especially outgoing, but we gravitated toward one another. As it turned out, we shared a love for books—not just class assignments—but reading for the sheer enjoyment of it. I had been reading *The Trilogy of Studs Lonigan*, which was about a tough Chicago Irish kid growing up on the South Side. Eleni was enamored of *How Green Was My Valley*, a coming-of-age tale from across the pond, set in a hardscrabble Welsh hamlet of coal miners.

Our supervisors soon realized that Eleni and I were becoming an item, so whenever we worked the same shift, they would give us our lunch breaks at the same time. Now that's something that would never happen at a chain supermarket like Jewel or Kroger. Broadway Finer Foods was at its finest for me.

It was early May, and we were enjoying unseasonably warm weather—75 degrees. All of Chicago was out and about enjoying Mother Nature. Not a soul was grocery shopping, except for a grizzled neighborhood elder who would pinch all the fruit but only buy a single plum. So our bosses granted us a full hour break, instead of the normal thirty minutes.

Lincoln Park was only a few blocks from the supermarket, and it beckoned. Eleni and I would stake out a park bench and hopefully enjoy some innocent cuddling, or necking, as it was known back in the sixties. Wild lovemaking was never my thing. And Eleni was no lustful tigress. So we were well matched.

We sat comfortably together with our backs to the city, on one of the park's iconic benches with wide, green horizontal slats bolted onto brackets made of concrete, solid enough to support a pair of grizzlies. Fortunately, neither of us was a grizzly nor a tiger. I gently wrapped my arm around her shoulder and leaned into her. I sensed she was a little uncomfortable.

"Hey Eleni, are you okay?"

"Uh—I'm all right—but, I have a confession to make."

After a pause that seemed to last for an eternity, she whispered, "I like girls."

Now it was my turn to pause. I was at a loss for words. I hadn't considered this as a possibility. Finally, I just blurted out, "It's okay, Eleni, I forgive you."

I forgive you? What did I know? Coming of age in an urban bubble in 1963, I had so much to learn.

To this very day, I marvel at Eleni's bravery, outing herself to me in 1963. Her trust in me made an enduring impression. She must have realized that I'd never betray that trust. Throughout the summer, we remained an "item" to everyone, but us. In the meantime, we both graduated from high school. Neither of us was into the prom scene, nor cared about school spirit, but we were okay with that. We had our own club of two and we liked it that way.

At summer's end, we went our separate ways. Eleni enrolled at the University of Illinois, downstate in Champaign. I remained in Chicago, registering at the University of Illinois' Chicago branch, otherwise known as Navy Pier or "Champaign On The Rocks." We exchanged letters for several months, but bit by bit, our correspondence just petered out.

Still, I never forgot Eleni nor that summer we were "dating." Nor have I forgotten how much we cared for and understood one another. And she trusted me with her secret! Our mutual love was unconventional in that era, yet still cherished.

In 2013, I sought Eleni on Facebook. Because she hadn't changed her name, she was easy to find. We exchanged greetings. She and her partner, Leah, were both comfortably ensconced as tenured professors at a small liberal arts college in Massachusetts. Earlier that year, they had tied the matrimonial knot, the very same year that gay marriage was legalized in that state—among the first in the nation.

Happy end!

***

A lifelong city kid, **Dan Terkell** has been an eyewitness to and participant in the urban circus that is Chicago since the 1950s. Having stumbled into Chicago's vibrant community of storytellers in late 2012, Dan has performed at various venues throughout the Chicago area.

During his lengthy work-life, he's held straight jobs, including budget analyst and planner, copywriter, and many eras ago, a bus pilot for the Chicago Transit Authority.

A shameless, bleeding-heart liberal, Dan is the creator of a politically fueled blog named *Hardwired to Reason* (hardwiredtoreason. blogspot.com). It's been dormant since January 2021, but he's determined to revive it.

Chapter 28 | Katy's Lonely Longing for Love by John Zimmerman

After twenty-five years as a newspaper writer, I returned to the special-education classroom. This time, my role was to train young disabled adults for jobs, and then to help them find work. That is when I met Katy. She was one of my best trainees, and just a swell human being.

Katy had a host of medical problems; she lost most of her vision over the years. But she could see the good in everyone. You knew it by the way she addressed her schoolmates when she burst into a classroom in her joyful, boisterous way.

"Good morning, good morning, good morning—it is a good morning!" she would say.

"Hey, don't get down… you're doing fine. You know how to do this," she would tell a classmate if that person was having difficulty with an assignment.

"I like what you say. I like how you laugh. I like how you sing," I heard her say many times to friends and teachers.

Katy would tap a merry tune with her cane as she made her way through the classroom, cheering on her peers and flashing her mile-wide smile. However, you didn't want to cross her. She would let you know your offense quickly, but she would be quick to forgive. Katy also had a wicked sense of humor.

"Mr. Z," she once said, "You're okay, but sometimes you talk too much. And that's hard on people whose ears are better than their eyes, you know!"

Katy wasn't about to let her near blindness and failing health stop her from getting a job or doing anything else she wanted to do. She always felt that way.

Until that one day, she didn't. I could tell she wasn't herself that morning at the restaurant where she was being trained for a job. She barely said hello as she sat down across from me at the booth. Her face was dipped in misery.

"You okay?" I asked.

"Fine," she replied with sad apathy.

"You don't seem fine, Katy."

"I said I'm fine!" she slammed her fist on the table for emphasis and immediately apologized. "I just want to do my work, okay, Mr. Z?"

I let her be—until she started making mistakes. That wasn't Katy. The teacher in me took over.

"Katy, you know at a real job, you wouldn't be able to come in to work like this."

"Like what?"

"In this mood. Doing your work wrong. You know that's not you. Please tell me what's wrong."

Then she cried. The big tears, the ones she was fighting to hold back, but couldn't because they were just too heavy, and they fell down her cheeks and onto her hands that were wrapped tightly around her folded cane.

"I want to be in love, Mr. Z."

I wasn't expecting that. I didn't know where it came from. When you are with young people with special needs, you hear and see just about everything. And you're ready with a response. But that time, I struggled for the right reply. She broke the embarrassing silence with a clarification.

"No, I don't want to be in love," she said. "I know how to be in love. I just want somebody to love me back."

I reached across the booth and took her hands.

"Lots of people love you, and love you back, like me."

"Not in the way I want to be loved," she said.

"Some guy is going to be very lucky to have a girlfriend like you," I said, in my best everything-is-going-to-be-okay tone.

Katy pulled her hands free and shot me a hard look.

"I trust in you, Mr. Z," she said, "because you told me you would never lie to me. But you just did. There ain't going to be nobody picking me up for dates. There ain't going to be nobody holding me in his arms. There ain't going to be nobody making out with me. There ain't going to be nobody wanting to marry me. I don't know what God was thinking when he made me. Made me sick, made me blind, though I see good enough to know what I look like. He made me ugly, too. Why? I don't know. I do know God has never answered my prayer to be beautiful."

"Stop it. You are beautiful," I said.

She wiped away her tears, shook her head, and said, "You're full of shit. Stop lying, Mr. Z," she said. "I know you're doing it to make me feel better, but it ain't working. There's no boy going to want to marry a girl like me. And there's not a pretty girl that would gladly trade places with me, which is what I want more than anything in the whole world."

I felt awful that she felt that way. And angry. I wanted to change her mind; to say something that she could believe and that would make her feel better. Katy saved me from the struggle by suddenly breaking out in a big laugh.

"I was just kidding, Mr. Z," she said, as she started correctly folding silverware into the white cloth napkins. "Just kidding!"

Of course, she wasn't.

We never brought up that moment again. I eventually left the program, and Katy graduated shortly thereafter. We texted for a while, but it wasn't the same as being together five days a week in the classroom. We eventually lost touch.

I never forgot Katy. I thought about her many times over the past years. I'd like to think that Katy found someone to share her life with. That someone did find her beautiful, inside and out. That her disability didn't matter. That her looks didn't matter. That is the way it should be. I wanted that so much for Katy.

That day in the restaurant, I wished I had a magic wand so I could turn Katy into a Disney Princess. She would pick up the phone on Friday night and hear the nervous boy at the other end, risking the pain of rejection by asking this beautiful young lady for a date. And she would giggle a yes. And the first date would lead to many more—all the way to the altar. I can imagine her beautiful face in the mirror smiling on that wedding day. And she would thank God for answering her prayer and giving her someone who truly loved her.

You know, we use words like "special" in talking about the disabled. *Special*? They're just like the rest of us who want a love that leads to a life together.

***

John Zimmerman is a retired journalist and teacher who lives in Carol Stream, IL. He was a writer and editor at two newspapers, including the Daily Herald in suburban Chicago. John won several awards, including an Indiana Associated Press first place in editorial writing, and an Illinois Press Association second place in column writing. John also taught special education and was a job coach for adults with special needs.

John is a playwright. His first play, *Artie Diaz Jackson Discovers America,* appeared in the Chicago Arc Theatre's New Works Festival in 2017. John has since had plays produced in California, Michigan, and New York. John has also tried his hand at acting. His favorite role was Pa Joad in the Infamous Commonwealth Theatre's production of *The Grapes of Wrath* at the Raven Theatre in Chicago.

John enjoys spending time with family. His grandchildren are a joy. John is also a grateful cancer survivor.

He thanks Chicago Story Press for believing in what sweet Katy had to say.

Chapter 29 | Waiting for Phil by David Barish

Today is Mother's Day and we are celebrating my mom, my wife, this special day, plummeting levels of new Covid cases, as well as our fully vaccinated status. An hour ago, my daughter, wife, and mother were nibbling on food we hoped to share with my brother, Phil. He was delayed. Delay is a thing with him. Is it because he is a musician, a late-night person, a guy married to a woman who likes to work out late in the afternoon, or because he lives out in the boondocks? I don't know and I don't care. He is always late. It's simply who he is. I have no judgement. I think that is part of the love language between Phil and me. We may roll our eyes at each other privately, but we don't judge publicly. Neither of us would want to live the life of the other, but we laugh at the same jokes, love the same music, have the same social and political views, and love each other intensely. The rest of my family cannot help being angry. My daughter is irked that he is late because she worked hard on this Mother's Day meal. My mother wants to call him. I know there is no point in calling and I say, "He will get here when he gets here."

This is an old issue newly arisen because we have not had family events for so long. Over the years, there has been a debate over whether to wait for Phil and risk the food getting cold or to serve before his arrival. Some family members want to start on time, others want to wait for Phil. I bounce between these poles depending on what we are serving, how many people are waiting, and how delayed he is going to be.

I have only seen my baby brother once since the Shelter-in-Place Order kept us stuck inside. Our refuge became our cell. We had a brief interlude sitting on his front porch for a single beer and attempted to cover too much ground in a short visit. We were not ready to hug each other, shake hands, or even get remotely close. Neither of us is a chatterbox on the phone, so we have spoken little, but it was still great to see him.

We usually celebrate each other's birthdays by going to hear music or attending a ballgame. In early January of last year, when there were a few isolated cases of this unusual virus, Phil took me out for my birthday. He is a musician, has a degree in Music Composition, and writes beautiful jazz. Aside from loving him as a brother, I love to hear him talk about music. He has a blend of art and science and can talk all night about inspiration and execution.

That night, we listened to some local musicians play sets of Herbie Hancock's complex and beautiful music. We talked about getting back to the venue on Chicago's South Side and wanting to hear more music together. But we didn't. I never got to reciprocate by taking Phil out for his birthday.

This will be the first family event Phil has attended in over a year.

He finally arrives forty-five minutes late. I greet him in my daughter's dining room and deeply hug my brother Phil. We have not hugged each other since March 2020 when the world changed and we all retreated to our lairs, masked, hidden, and afraid. But now, Phil and I hold each other tightly. We let the moment linger. I can hear my mother and my daughter talking, a dog barking outside, some cars on nearby streets, but I return my focus to digging in and holding on. I am trying to catch up on over a year's worth of hugs.

After our long hug and reconnection, he gets himself a plate of food and sits in the living room, catching up with everybody. He advises my wife about sound issues. She is interested in doing a recording of herself reading her just published book. Phil, who has a degree in music composition and a sound lab in his home, is a maven about music but also about sound and recording. He is a self-taught engineer. The discussion of recording is deep. The rest of us listen as they talk about how he will help her navigate the idiosyncrasies of Amazon's Audible platform.

Their discussion loosens us up and we all talk. The conversation is freewheeling. We exchange jokes, we laugh, and we gently rib each other. Everybody sits back and smiles and then talks for several more hours.

We are not going back to the life we had before the pandemic. I will get to hug Phil again, but we will not sit in a crowded club or filled ballpark together for our birthdays. I suspect we will eat a meal outdoors. I will invite him to my home, and he and his wife might come. I wish this pandemic was over. I'll take what I can get, but I want more.

I want to wait for Phil to arrive. I want to look at my watch, roll my eyes, and look at my phone, but not call him. I want to worry we are going to miss the beginning of a show, and I want to get the stink eye from my mom, or my wife, or one of my daughters as they see me wait by the front door for him looking like a little boy awaiting the bus on the first day of school.

I want to pull out my credit card to pay for the first round of drinks and order a couple of snifters of Laphroaig neat. I want my heart rate finally to simmer down, as we get to the venue barely in time to hear the band. I want to sip that drink and listen to him tell me about a recording he has of the bass player's band, and I want to hear him tell me about the music he is writing.

I don't want to see Phil and his wife in one little square on my computer, distracted by their barking dogs. I need Phil live, in the flesh, where I can hug him and where he can feel what I am experiencing in this moment, and for him to know how special he is to me even though we have not seen enough of each other.

I can wait all day for Phil to show up, but I can't wait any more days for him to do so.

***

David Barish's stories have been published in Story Club Magazine, *Chicago Storytellers from Stage to Page*, and Stitch. He has told stories at venues all over the Chicago area and has co-hosted an open mic for storytellers for several years. He is an attorney who represents injured workers and Social Security Disability claimants.

Chapter 30 | He Stole My Heart by Debbi Welch

In 2010, my oldest brother, Mark, started having trouble with his heart. He was scheduled for surgery to repair a valve, and I was to fly into my hometown of Pittsfield, Massachusetts to help take care of him after he was released from the hospital. Things didn't go as planned. It started with a valve replacement instead of a simple repair—longer surgery and lots of anesthesia.

I have so many wonderful memories of Mark. When I was twelve, he joined the Navy. He was gone for what seemed like forever. Almost every week a postcard would arrive, addressed to me, from some far-off place—some I'd never even heard of. He'd tell me about what he was doing on the ship, and the places he and his friends had visited, but would always find the space to ask something about me. "How was I doing in school? What had I been up to?" One week there was no postcard. There was a package from Spain! I tried to imagine what would be in the box. I tore it open and found a royal blue fringed bikini. Now remember, I was twelve and my bra size was nonexistent.

My mom was aghast. "How could your brother send you something so inappropriate?"

I felt just the opposite. I was so proud and delighted that Mark did that. I felt grown up and important. My brother thought I was a match for a royal blue fringed bikini. Wow! Looking back at it now, I'm sure he did it just for fun. I never wore it, but it was a treasured possession.

I missed Mark so much while he was gone. I'd read those postcards over and over and look up the places he had been, so that I could feel even closer to him. When he finally came home for good, he brought me something else to wear—a navy pea coat. It was a bit too big, but it didn't matter. I felt like a million bucks in it and wore that coat for many years.

After my plane landed, I made my way to Pittsfield and over the next couple of days, my sister-in-law, Mary, and I would drive two hours each day to the hospital and back. The hospital had her cell-phone number, so we never worried that she couldn't be reached in an emergency. On my third day there, we drove home and had a relaxed dinner. Then Mary checked her house voicemail. I watched her face turn white as she began to cry.

"What are they saying? What's wrong?" I kept asking.

"All the message says is that we need to get back to the hospital right away. No explanation—nothing. That's it."

Mary tried to reach someone at the hospital but couldn't find out anything. We raced there and found out that a nurse's aide had helped Mark to stand and then moved away from him. While she wasn't looking at or supporting him, he coded—his heart stopped—and he fell to the floor, hitting his head on the way down. No one was there to catch him.

I wished I had been there to catch him—the way he caught me when I was eight. Mark taught me how to ride a bike because my father did little positive parenting. Day after day, Mark would hold my bike steady so that I could get on and fit my feet to the pedals, which were also my brakes. Then he would give me a push. I grew up in Western Massachusetts, a land of many hills and mountains. My house was at the top of a hill, and the end of my street was at the bottom. No one wore helmets, elbow pads, or knee pads.

Mark would run along beside me, giving me encouragement, and reminding me to keep the handlebars straight. Just before I got to the end of the block, he would yell, "Brakes!" and I would push really hard on the pedals and come to a stop.

One day we went through our usual take-off checklist.

"Feet on pedals," he said.

"Check," I responded.

"Handlebars straight."

"Check."

"Bike pointed toward Elm Street."

"Check."

Elm Street was the busiest in our neighborhood.

Mark gave me a push, and I started down the block, gaining momentum. I could see the neighbors' houses as I went whooshing by faster and faster. I wanted to wave to Mrs. McKenna when I went past but was too scared to lift my hand off the handlebar. So I gave her a nod and a smile and continued on my way.

And then my feet slipped off the pedals. I tried to get them back on but couldn't coordinate my feet and the pedals. I screamed as I headed for the intersection filled with traffic.

And then, there he was, my knight in shining armor—my big brother—jumping in front of my bike, catching me, and stopping me a few feet short of entering traffic. We both ended up on the ground. He was sweaty and totally out of breath. I was crying and bloody, having cut up both of my knees.

We rested for a few minutes and then walked back up the street. As soon as my knees were cleaned up and bandaged, Mark got me back up on the bike and we tried it once again. I wasn't afraid to try again because I knew he'd be there to catch me.

And now Mark had fallen, and no one had been there to catch him. After he flatlined, they revived him. He had suffered a severe concussion, and his stay in the hospital was extended yet again.

Between all the anesthesia and the concussion, he didn't always recognize me. Because he usually fell asleep watching a foreign-language channel, he often woke up thinking he was in Japan. That passed, but the confusion and memory lapses took quite a while to disappear.

Mark was still in the hospital when I had to fly back to Chicago. Before I left, I helped my sister-in-law by cooking some meals to freeze, cleaning the house, and visiting my brother while Mary got some rest. It never felt like enough—not after everything he'd done for me.

This is the man who taught me how to ride my bike and thought of me on at least a weekly basis when he was overseas. He also included me in his weeklong summer Monopoly games with his friends, took me fishing, and taught me how to bait my own hook, which was a big deal in our family.

This man's heart, pacemaker and all, is one of the biggest I've ever known. Mark has always had my back, and he stole my heart from the first minute I knew him.

***

Debbi Welch has been a storyteller and writer in Chicago for over thirty years. As a children's entertainer, Debbi has appeared in many venues including The Art Institute of Chicago, Second City Children's Theater, and the Chicago Public Libraries, and many public and private schools. She has performed her personal essays in Chicago, Seattle, and London.

Debbi is a board member emeritus and past president of the Board of Directors of Young Chicago Authors, an organization that helps young people from all backgrounds to understand the importance of their own stories and those of others. She created and coordinated the Authors in the Schools Program for the Chicago Near South Planning Board, bringing authors and their books into elementary schools across the city. Debbi also spent six years coordinating all the children's programming for the Printers Row Book Fair.

Debbi is the proud wife, mother, and mother-in-law of accomplished poets, essayists, and nonfiction writers. She is looking forward to hearing and reading the words and stories of her grandchildren.

Chapter 31 | Pigeon by Anna Tuccoli

When I was nineteen, I met "The One," or so I thought. I was impressed and flattered when he confessed he had been following me around campus, stalking me. I didn't notice him. So, maybe it wasn't really stalking. Karl approached me one day in the student lounge at college. I recognized him because we had been in a cultural geography course together. As we talked, we realized we had common intellectual interests and similar backgrounds; we were both the first generation to go to college with parents who were working class. Karl was a diligent worker who juggled a job at a local newspaper with a full-course load at college that included a significant commute. We made plans to go out that weekend.

Our first date was unlike any other dates I had. We went to a protest in Berkley at the University of California. In 1968 that is what people did. We raised our fists to "Viva Che" and listened to speeches. The cops broke up the event, so we visited his childhood friend, Jean. She was a student at Berkley who was running for President of the Student Body and strongly identified with Mao. She was only eighteen and her interest in politics was a lifetime passion. Much later, she became the Mayor of Oakland. As we sat in her apartment, we discussed radical-left politics and other things. When we left, I felt like I had been transformed, enlightened. All these ideas were heady stuff for a nineteen-year-old sheltered suburban girl.

My relationship with Karl progressed quickly. We studied together, and he helped me draft better papers, pass tests with high grades, and improve my scholarship. He was the first man with whom I had a sexual connection; this was no fleeting flirtation. He placed me on a pedestal, worshipped me, and told all his friends about me. We were so in love. Compared to my friends, I thought I was experiencing the best love

I could ever have. Upon graduation from college, we married at twenty-one in an outdoor wedding in a beautiful state park.

Karl decided to go to graduate school, and I supported the idea. He received a fellowship from Syracuse University. We packed up our old car with the few things we owned and moved three thousand miles to upstate New York. I thought it would be a great romantic adventure until my house of cards collapsed. There was nothing for me to do there. I wondered how much I misjudged everything in my life. The first year, I did nothing but babysit for professors' children. The second year, I received a fellowship as a teaching assistant in the Anthropology Department. A few years later, I finished with a master's degree that led to no gainful employment or career. Karl didn't finish his degree and quit to work at an alternative newspaper.

We had nothing, no money, no car, and no help from our relatives. We had so little money that we received food stamps. Things only improved slightly when Karl got another job. But I felt stranded with no family support, just a handful of friends, and Karl kept changing into someone I did not know. He was touchy, angry, and argumentative. He took on an air of arrogance that he was superior to me, ridiculing me in front of friends and mocking me as if anything I said was ridiculous and vapid. I was rebuked if I asked if he was depressed. "Quit bugging me. I give people ulcers, I don't have 'em."

When I tried to reason with him about borrowing money from our parents, he said, "Don't ask for help from family. I don't want them to know."

I was no longer the perfect girl on a pedestal, pursuing a romantic dream with the love of my life. The only power I had over my life was a kind of denial. I held on to a naïve illusion that everything was fine and that it would all work out. It took some years to come to a reckoning that Karl and I made each other puny. A change was about to come, and it began one stark winter.

I could not believe what I was witnessing. It stung me into a reality that I had tried to deny for so long.

***

I screamed when I saw the ruffled pigeon lying there on the cold cement ramp.

Still alive, it barely raised its shiny green-gray head. The silent warehouse ricocheted my screams as the car engine sounds overpowered the loudly cooing, flopping bird. I felt like he had run over me.

"You killed it," I said. "Can't you watch what you're doing?"

"Sorry," he said. "Didn't see it. It's not dead. Look, it's moving," my husband pointed at it.

"I think it's crippled. You crippled it. I have to go. This place makes me sick, anyway. It stinks. I have to go to work."

I glanced at the bird; it was blinking its ringed eyes every few seconds. It was obviously in pain. I hurried down the ramp and out the metal door, which slammed hard behind me.

The sidewalks of downtown Syracuse were mounded on the sides with four to five feet of snow. The snow was old, dirty, and yellowed in parts from dogs. The gray and black layers were frozen like stone. The gray morning without sun felt like every other winter morning there.

I felt sick. The bird's pain was imprinted in the pit of my stomach and my gut churned.

Karl always insisted on backing our tiny, hatchback silver Honda Civic up the ramp of the warehouse printing office. He worked for a wine company as a graphic artist, and he printed advertisements he designed and then dropped them off at grocery stores, wine sellers, and gourmet shops. He liked to back up so he could easily stack the flyers into the car for his distribution route around town.

The place had a peculiar mix of smells: acrid printing ink, hot grease from the press, and carbon monoxide exhaust fumes. I hated the stench, the filth, the unabating cold. He loved it.

I came back to the warehouse after work. The pigeon was still there, unable to move. I stared at it for a long while. I went into the clattering printing room to see if he could take me home. If the print run was almost done, I could be home in less than half an hour. But if not, I'd have a long, cold wait for the bus.

"Pigeon's still in the same place," I said.

"What pigeon?" he responded absent-mindedly.

"The one you ran over. It's dying."

"I got better things to worry about. The press broke down this afternoon. Just got it working."

"Oh… it's the bus I guess."

I stooped over the pigeon on my way out. Its wings hung down; its head was tucked over its side. It awakened, blinked, and tried to move but could not. It was paralyzed, maybe a broken back.

The next morning it was still there, and it barely blinked when I came up. It cooed weakly.

At lunch time I felt compelled to check on it again. Not much change. I wished it would die. I felt miserable. I argued as usual with Karl. I was two months pregnant, and he didn't want children.

"That pigeon is dying out there. It's suffering."

"Okay. I'll fix that," he said as he grabbed a pair of long-bladed scissors used for page layouts.

The scissors flashed open. Karl sunk the blade deep into the pigeon's back. He wiped the blood off the blade with an old dirty rag. The pigeon flopped to its side, eyes closed. I ran and vomited into a dirty little toilet in the warehouse.

I slunk back to my stupid office job, which mostly involved copying and filing things. It paid next to nothing. I had little in common with anyone there. As I tried to work, my stomach churned, and I couldn't eat without vomiting. At the end of the day, I didn't even bother to stop to see if I could get a ride from my husband. I took the bus home. I made some soup and went to sleep thinking about the poor pigeon's death.

The next day, we exchanged pleasantries in the morning on the way to work. Karl invited me to have lunch with him, which was a welcome change from sitting in the lonely staff lunchroom at work.

I brought my bag lunch but felt afraid to eat much. The acrid odor filled the air, and the dead pigeon lay on the ramp. The flies were buzzing around it. I tried to ignore all of this. We ate some of the lunch and then the conversation turned to finances. The topic always roiled my stomach.

Karl launched into his usual, "You know money's tight? Right? That piddly-ass-little job of yours doesn't pay much more than the phone and utility bills. I don't think we can make it with that, do you?"

"Look, I'm trying my best here."

I felt ashamed that I couldn't do better even with two college degrees.

Karl continued, "So, I think we need to consider that this pregnancy isn't anything we can afford, right?" His voice was forceful, authoritative.

"What do you mean?" I said, as I started to cry. I felt sick again.

"Abortion's legal, isn't it?" he said. "You know I don't want any kids. Diabetes, that's not something for a kid to inherit."

It was true, Karl and his brother had both inherited Type I Diabetes. Given the genetic testing technology of the late 1970s there was no way to know if it would be passed on to our children.

"You don't know that," I said as the tears came down my cheeks. "I have to leave."

Later that evening we had another bitter discussion about going to Planned Parenthood to discuss terminating my pregnancy. I cried myself to sleep.

The next morning, I made an appointment with the clinic, and they confirmed my pregnancy. I told Karl about the results, and he was furious. I didn't ask about options. I decided not to argue. That day, I received an acceptance letter from the University of Chicago for graduate school in social work with a small scholarship. I showed him the letter.

It surprised me when he said, "You see. You can't go to graduate school with a baby."

I steeled myself. A thousand arguments went through my mind. I felt stunned and pressured, torn between a rock and a hard place. I cried and pleaded with Karl, who was unbending and would not listen. In the end, I knew I needed to change my life for the better. I reluctantly went through with ending my pregnancy. Afterward, I felt depressed and numb. I missed so much work, they fired me.

I didn't go to graduate school that year because Karl wasn't "ready to move." I got a better job in the area. But as things improved financially, I grew more disenchanted with my husband. I grew resentful, angry, and disinterested in my marriage. I didn't admit it fully to myself then. My feelings showed themselves in many small ways. I would go out with new friends from work, ignoring Karl and rarely spending time with him, having petty arguments when I did. I applied again for graduate school the next year, and this time I accepted the offer from the University of Chicago. Karl acted as if he was planning to leave with me but did little to prepare for the actual move to Chicago.

On my thirtieth birthday, I moved to Chicago. Karl helped me move and said he would follow, but he never did. I was on my own for the first time in my life in a strange city. It was a hellish adjustment with doubts, bouts of loneliness, depression, grief, and several identity crises. Two years later, I graduated with a master's degree in social work and a brand-new profession that lasted over thirty years. Most importantly, I learned to fail and get up again, to be independent, to love who I was, and to believe in what I could accomplish.

The image of that poor pigeon who could not move and was in pain has stayed with me for all these years. Although I didn't recognize it then, I remember the look in its eyes and the sense of wanting to live and endure, to fly.

***

Anna Tuccoli holds a master's degree in social work from the University of Chicago. She is a semi-retired licensed clinical social worker who has worked most of her career with children and families. As a social worker, Anna deeply listens to the stories of others. In fact, she calls them the "greatest stories never told." She has decided it is time to tell her own stories. She has been published in an anthology of storytellers, *Chicago Storytellers From Stage to Page,* by Chicago Story Press. She has performed two of her stories at the renowned Newberry Library in 2020 and 2021, and at the Chicago Park District in 2020. When not writing, Anna loves to read, take art classes, dance, and hike. She resides in Chicago with her husband and dog.

Chapter 32 | Therapy by Steve Glickman

Many years ago, before Covid, I'm working late at the office one night. I call my partner Greg to let him know I won't be home until midnight. He tells me he's going out for drinks with a friend, so he'll see me later.

That might sound like a normal conversation between domestic partners of seven years, except that it's Valentine's Day. Greg and I haven't exchanged flowers or cards, we have no plans for dinner or a date-night. We're both pretending Valentine's Day isn't happening because it's easier than facing the truth.

A week later we have a difficult conversation and we break-up. A month later, Greg moves out. And that's a wrap: seven years. The weird thing is I still love him, but it just wasn't working. Suddenly, I am very lonely.

I call up a new guy, a friend of a friend, someone who I've wondered about and flirted with occasionally. We talk on the phone for a while, then I casually drop into the conversation that I'm newly single.

A few weeks later, I'm at the new guy's apartment on our first date. He cooks a beautiful dinner, candles and flowers, the whole bit. After dinner we're sitting on his sofa side by side, sipping some wine, inching closer and closer. He looks into my eyes, and I return his gaze, inviting him in. He kisses me, and I kiss him back. It feels amazing to kiss someone new after seven years. I close my eyes and give in to the passion.

Then suddenly, I see Greg in my mind's eye staring back at me, as if to say, "How dare you!"

I pull away and say, "I can't do this. It's too soon. I'm sorry."

***

A week later, I'm in therapy. It's my first time trying this, on the advice of a friend. The therapist, Don, is an older gay man (I hope older and wiser). In his office, there's a sofa for me and a chair for him, and a Kleenex box on a little side table, I'm guessing for me. Don wears a cardigan sweater and takes careful notes.

In our first few sessions, I confess this wasn't my first seven-year relationship; there was another one before this. I am a seven-year relationship ender. It's a pattern.

Don eventually asks if I see any similarities between the two relationships.

"Yes, there were many," I say. "But most notably, from the start of both relationships, I had doubts. I put up with far too much for way too long. I'm not sure why, but I think it's because I'm scared of being alone."

"Why is that?" Don asks.

"When I was in high school, I had no friends. I didn't participate in sports or clubs. I had no social life. All I cared about was academics. I got straight A's and was a classic smarty-pants. "A" for arrogant. I thought, *I don't need friends, I don't have time for idle play, I am destined for greatness.* I remember sitting in class on Monday mornings and hearing about all the parties that happened over the weekend, who was dating whom, etc., and thinking, *I'm not a part of that.*

"Hmm. What do you think now?"

"Turns out I was wrong. I do need friends. I actually like people. I was just a lonely, closeted, gay kid trying to navigate high school back in the seventies. I've learned a lot since then. But to this day, I'm terrified of being alone on a Saturday night. I think maybe it's why I've stayed with the wrong guys for too long."

"High school was a long time ago, "Don says. "How about we face this monster in your closet?"

We hatch a plan. I'm going to spend an entire weekend in my apartment alone—no contact with anyone. And I'm going to survive by filling my time with things I love to do.

As the weekend approaches, I make a to-do list because it comforts me. I'm tempted to call a friend, but somehow, I resist.

The weekend arrives. On Saturday morning, I make banana-walnut pancakes, my favorite. Then I watch my favorite movie, *Fiddler on the Roof.* Twice! I take a long walk in a lovely park nearby. When I return home, I see my to-do list sitting on a table and I put it in a drawer. Then I take a nice long nap.

For dinner, I learn how to cook a new dish, pasta primavera. I set the table properly with flowers and cloth napkins. I sit down by myself. I think about all the parties, concerts, and dinner dates happening right now that I'm not a part of. And I realize I'm going to be okay. I take a bite of the pasta. It tastes pretty good but needs more spice, and I make a mental note for next time.

After dinner, I draw a bath, and not just any bath: a bubble bath, with little floating candles, and dim lighting, and Mozart playing softly on the stereo. Ahh.

This was the beginning of my journey in therapy. Over the next two years, Don helped me face more monsters in my closet, some of them bigger and scarier. More important than any single monster were the weapons he gave me to face them. I learned how to keep a journal. I learned how to set my boundaries and respect those of others. I learned how to accept rejection graciously. I learned how to be kind to myself, how to forgive myself, and how to love myself. And I like to think I became a little less arrogant.

At my last therapy session, there wasn't much left to say. I looked at Don and said, "Thank you for saving my life."

***

Fifteen years later, I live with Mark, my life-partner. He's the one for me. I have no doubts. And while Mark and I get along great, our relationship is far from perfect. We have occasional misunderstandings like any couple. But I address them head-on using the tools that Don gave me.

Last Valentine's Day, Mark gave me a bouquet of flowers and I gave him a sappy Hallmark card. We cooked a simple dinner together. After dinner, Mark went to bed early, as he often does. I'm the night owl. I lit a candle, turned on some soft music, and drew a bubble bath.

***

Steve Glickman's stories have been featured on The Moth Radio Hour and podcast. He's performed at the Laugh Factory, City Winery, and many other Chicago venues. Before Covid, he hosted the monthly storytelling show, Do Not Submit in Chicago's Edgewater neighborhood. He's performed with the Piven Theater, Tellin' Tales Theater, the Evanston Storytelling Festival, This Much Is True, Story Sessions, You're Being Ridiculous, First Person Live, Story Jam, Story Club, Truth or Lie, Tenx9, and others.

By day, he's a software engineer. He earned his bachelor's degree from the University of Illinois at Urbana-Champaign with a major in computer science and a minor in music. He lives in the Uptown neighborhood of Chicago with his partner Mark and their imaginary dog Ruffles. You can learn more about Steve on his website: steveglickman.net

Chapter 33 | A Loving Spirit by Madeleine Holden

It's late August, always such a busy time, not a moment to think about anything. Today's the first day of ninth grade for my daughter Evelyn, and I have a few uninterrupted hours to deal with the heaviness in my heart. As I head out in my electric wheelchair, I wave to my husband Jean-Pierre, on his tractor. He's working in the upper field and waves back. I point down the dirt road towards the lower field to show where I'm going. He nods, gives me the thumbs up, and blows me a kiss. He knows if I don't come back after awhile, where to look for me.

I'm going to the pond. It's one of my favorite places on our land. It wasn't always a pond, more like a depression in the lower field where farm equipment would get stuck in the mud. We brought in an excavator and a bulldozer to solve the problem. We dug it out and made a dam. Now it's filled with water and all the vegetation has grown back. I love it here. It's where I contemplate the infinitely large and the infinitely small. I watch the dragonflies land on the bulrushes swaying in the wind. I watch a family of ducks hide under the reeds. I look down and see the bees drink from the water in the pond. And I let myself feel the sadness of losing my friend Nancy to breast cancer at the beginning of this month.

I met Nancy in French class when I was twelve years old. I was drawn to her from the very first moment. Nancy had dark brown eyes and long brown hair with bangs cut short. She was a little gangly in her movements, dressed in jeans and moccasins with a patterned peasant blouse with purple beads hanging down. She looked like my kind of girl. From opposite sides of the class, she looked at me, laughing so hard with the French girls she had tears in her eyes, and I knew she wanted me to be part of her inside joke and inner circle. It was her smile that drew me into her sphere.

We grew up with a shared obsession for Chris de Burgh's album, *Spanish Train and Other Stories*. When we would get together, we would sing and dance like our lives depended on it. The lyrics of the song, *Old Friend* became the soundtrack of our lives. We saw him in concert at the Forum in Montreal and sang it together. We went for walks in the dark around town or up on the mountain and sang, feeling safe because we had each other. "Old friend, so you're in trouble again," a lyric from our favorite song, was our mantra of unconditional support.

Life could be so messy. No matter what was happening in our lives, whether it was tragic or filled with joy, our deep love for each other committed us for life. Accidents and breakups, weddings, and baptisms: Nancy was present for them all as an integral part of my family—a sister, a friend, the fun-filled aunty. Even though we were separated by distance and the business of busy lives, when we were together, it was as if no time had passed. With that much love, picking up where we left off was as natural as the sun rising and setting daily and as reliable as the changing of the seasons.

Nancy was the embodiment of a loving spirit. Always at the center of a social gathering as organizer or event planner, always giving of herself to make others feel special. But it was the private moments with her I loved the most. I watched her as she sat in her rocking chair in the sunny corner of her living room, with a twin daughter in each arm sleeping. This silence felt sacred. We talked quietly about motherhood and the pressure women feel to have it all, to do it all, to be it all. Even back then she said wisely, "I wish there was more time."

One day in late September, my old friend confided that she was in trouble again. We were having lunch on an outdoor patio at a restaurant at the base of our mountain. Soaking up the fall sunshine, we reminisced about our youthful shenanigans and boundless energy. Then she looked at me, her blonde streaks and wild feathered hair blowing in the breeze and said, "I have cancer, but they caught it early, and I am going to fight this and win." And I believed her because the alternative was unfathomable.

I saw her at the funeral for the mother of a mutual friend in late July. I can still feel the weight of her hand on my shoulder. In a room full of people, she squeezed my hand and whispered in my ear, "I have to go. I'm so tired." Those were the last words she ever said to me and the last time I saw her. Just six days later, she was gone. My prayers were full of sadness and loss until I tried to focus on the happy times. She had lived a life worth celebrating.

I recalled how we had a Saint-Jean-Baptiste bonfire just up the hill at the beginning of summer with a group of friends. She was so funny, just vibrating with life. She had been swimming at the civic center all winter and looked strong. She called out, "Aubergiste!" when her glass was empty, but instead of waiting to be served by the imaginary innkeeper, she jumped up and happily filled everyone's glass. That image of Nancy filling my glass that was already half-full with the last drops of red wine, the glow from the fire making her skin and smile shine brightly, filled me with joy. She had finished a year of treatments, her hair was just starting to grow back, and we thought she had beaten the cancer. She would want me to remember her like this.

I look at my watch and realize hours have passed. It's time to get back to the house and see my daughter, who will arrive home soon. I don't want to miss the stories of her first day, her teachers, her classes, and hear what everybody did all summer. I turn to head back up the field, and I hear a muffled thud as my front wheel falls into a hole, and I am suddenly, violently ejected out of my chair, and I somersault to the ground. I am now lying flat on my back in the hay field beside the pond with a brand-new perspective, feeling tiny, looking up into the heavens above. It is hard to fall lower than the ground.

My heart is pounding so fast. *What if I broke something? What if I'm injured? What if I landed on a wasp nest? Or an anthill? What if I slip into the pond and drown?*

I panic. I had to stop these crazy thoughts. I glance over and see the edge of the pond several feet away. I know I would not drown. I look at my feet and see no awkward angles; nothing is broken. I am okay. I just need to control my emotions. *Think Zen thoughts. I can do this.*

I take a deep breath and exhale slowly. I feel the warm sun on my body, the breeze on my face. Far above, two hawks circle in the bright blue sky. And that is when I hear Nancy's laugh. She *would* think this is funny. On a long blade of grass, a grasshopper watched me. I feel Nancy is there. I feel her presence. I close my eyes to enjoy her closeness.

So, what's the story here, Madeleine? Having a little pity party?

"I just want to spend some time with you," I whisper into the wind.

You are going to have to be more careful. We're not invincible, just human. This chair has a seatbelt, and it's not just for holding babies on your lap while you bomb around town. And you don't even own a cellphone! What are you thinking? You need to be smart here when you take off cross-country alone.

"I know. I will," I reply.

And find someone to tell your stories to. Don't leave secrets to fester inside. That can make you sick. Tell your stories, even the dark ones, especially the dark ones. You will feel so much better. Now, wake up! Your Zen thoughts have put you to sleep!

As I resurface from my dream, I hear my voice say out loud, "I miss you. I love you."

And I hear Nancy's response, *Be brave, I'll be with you. I'll always be with you.*

I hear rustling in the grass. My saviors have come down on their bikes. Jean-Pierre and Evelyn pick me up and put me back in my chair. I head back home between them while Evelyn chats about her day. My heart is no longer heavy. It is filled with the light, loving spirit of my friend Nancy, and a plan to tell our stories to anyone who will listen.

***

Madeleine Holden is a new author. She discovered storytelling in November 2020 when she took a workshop on a whim, searching to break the isolation of confinement of the global pandemic, Covid. Since then, she has performed live on virtual stages for Bodies of Stories and Soul Stories Live. She has been a featured guest on the podcast, *The Volume Knob—The Songs That Saved Your Life*. Her story, *Indelible Ink*, will soon be available on Amazon.

She lives in St. Isidore, Quebec, on a small farm with her husband, Jean-Pierre. She is a mentor to her peers for Mémo-Québec, in her region of Chaudière-Appalaches.

About the Editor | Anne E Beall, PhD

Anne is a writer and storyteller who has written nine books. She has been interviewed on NPR about her book *Heroic, Helpful & Caring Cats*, and her book *Cinderella Didn't Live Happily Ever After* was featured in *People Magazine*. Her other books include *Words of Encouragement; 5-Minute Sleep Meditations; 5-Minute Meditation Vacations; Community Cats, Heartfelt Connections; Strategic Market Research;* and *Reading the Hidden Communications Around You.*

She has told stories all over Chicago in a variety of shows, including Story Lab, Ten by Nine, Is This a Thing, Soul Stories, and The Moth. She is the CEO and founder of Beall Research, a strategic market research firm. She holds a PhD in social psychology from Yale University.

Originally from Massachusetts, she's lived in Chicago for over twenty years and enjoys walking on the lakefront, sampling dark beers, and listening to other storytellers.

About the Editor | Judi Lee Goshen

Judi is a writer, actor, and storyteller. Her book *Fornicationally Challenged:My Reluctant Return to Dating*, received a Readers' Favorite Award as well as one of the Top 100 Notable Books by Shelf Unbound. She also co-edited *Chicago Storytellers From Stage to Page*. She has been published in Beyond Words Literary Magazine, The South Loop Review, and Story Salon. Several of her screenplays and teleplays have garnered recognition from Writer's Digest and The Slamdance Competitions.

As a Moth winning storyteller, Judi has written and told hundreds of stories including her comedic one-woman show: *Fornicationally Challenged*, which was directed by Mark Travis.

Her free time, and her heart, belong to her two grandchildren.

Acknowledgements

This book would not be possible without the talented collection of storytellers who submitted their stories. These authors make this book funny, heartwarming, and meaningful. It was a pleasure to work with all of you. We are grateful that you have shared a part of yourself through your story of love: Christa Avampato, David Barish, Tonya Clanton, Jacoby Cochran, Barrie Cole, Julie Danis, Jonathan Euseppi, Steve Glickman, Nestor Gomez, Louis Greenwald, John Hahm, Steven Hoffman, Madeleine Holden, Jill Howe, Jitesh Jaggi, Arlene Malinowski, Pamela Morgan, Tom Myers, Carmenita Peoples, Randy Richardson, JC Quigley, Sheri Reda, Maureen Riley, Bridget Schank, Patti Shaffner, Francesca Sobrer, Debra Taitel, Paul Teodo, Dan Terkell, Anna Tuccoli, Debbi Welch, and John Zimmerman. You have created a wonderful volume that delves into love in its many forms.

We also want to thank the talented Johnny An who created the cover for this book. Your design captured the feeling many of us have when we feel loved. And thank you to Lidia Hernandez, who updated the cover.

And thank you, reader, for picking up this volume.

Thank you and Feedback

Dear Reader,

Thank you so much for spending your time reading this book. We hope that you enjoyed these stories and found the tellers inspiring.

If you have feedback about the book, you can email us at ChicagoStoryPress@gmail.com. Whether you loved it or hated it, tell us what you think.

Finally, if you have a few minutes, it will help tremendously if you would write a quick review on Amazon.

Reviews make an enormous difference, and the more reviews a book receives, the more people will learn about it.

Thanks again,

Anne E. Beall & Judi Lee Goshen